COOKING WITH TROUT

COOKING WITH TROUT

CONSULTANT EDITOR
JANE BAMFORTH

LORENZ BOOKS

This edition is published by Lorenz Books
Lorenz Books is an imprint of Anness Publishing Ltd
Hermes House, 88–89 Blackfriars Road, London SE1 8HA
tel. 020 7401 2077; fax 020 7633 9499; www.lorenzbooks.com; info@anness.com

© Anness Publishing Ltd 2003

This edition distributed in the UK by The Manning Partnership Ltd
6 The Old Dairy, Melcombe Road, Bath BA2 3LR
tel. 01225 478 444; fax 01225 478 440; sales@manning-partnership.co.uk
This edition distributed in the USA and Canada by National Book Network
4720 Boston Way, Lanham, MD 20706; tel. 301 459 3366; fax 301 459 1705; www.nbnbooks.com
This edition distributed in Australia by Pan Macmillan Australia
Level 18, St Martins Tower, 31 Market St, Sydney, NSW 2000
tel. 1300 135 113; fax 1300 135 103; customer.service@macmillan.com.au
This edition distributed in New Zealand by David Bateman Ltd, 30 Tarndale Grove,
Off Bush Road, Albany, Auckland; tel. (09) 415 7664; fax (09) 415 8892

A CIP catalogue record for this book is available from the British Library.

PUBLISHER: Joanna Lorenz
MANAGING EDITOR: Judith Simons
PROJECT EDITOR: Sarah Ainley
COPY EDITOR: Jenni Fleetwood
REFERENCE SECTION: Jenni Fleetwood and Kate Whiteman
RECIPES: Catherine Atkinson, Alex Barker, Jane Bamforth, Carla Capalbo, Jacqueline Clarke,
Roz Denny, Matthew Drennan, Joanne Farrow, Christine France, Brian Glover, Becky Johnson,
Christine Ingram, Liz Trigg, Linda Tubby, Kate Whiteman and Elizabeth Wolfe-Cohen
PHOTOGRAPHY: Tim Auty, Martin Brigdale, Nicki Dowey, James Duncan, Michelle Garrett,
Dave Jordan, David King, Thomas Odulate, William Lingwood and Sam Stowell
ADDITIONAL PHOTOGRAPHY (pp8 and 9): The Anthony Blake Photo Library
DESIGNER: Adelle Morris
INDEXER: Helen Snaith

1 3 5 7 9 10 8 6 4 2

NOTES
Bracketed terms are intended for American readers.
For all recipes, quantities are given in both metric and imperial measures and, where appropriate, measures
are also given in standard cups and spoons. Follow one set, but not a mixture, because they are not
interchangeable. Standard spoon and cup measures are level. 1 tsp = 5ml, 1 tbsp = 15ml, 1 cup = 250ml/
8fl oz. Australian standard tablespoons are 20ml. Australian readers should use 3 tsp in place of 1 tbsp for
measuring small quantities. Medium (US large) eggs are used unless otherwise stated.

CONTENTS

INTRODUCTION

Lovely to look at, delicious and nutritious, trout makes it a pure pleasure to eat more fish.

Fresh trout can be served in dozens of different ways – poached, baked, steamed, fried,

grilled (broiled), cooked on the barbecue or in the microwave. Equally delicious hot or cold,

it also stars in soufflés, pâtés and mousses, pastries and pasta dishes, sandwiches and salads.

Trout can be smoked successfully, adding another dimension to its culinary possibilities.

The tasty, varied recipes in this book, coupled with all the advice on preparing and cooking,

will reveal the enormous versatility of this truly wonderful fish.

THE STORY OF TROUT

Catching a glimpse of quicksilver trout in a quiet pool or lake is one of the delights of the countryside. Not only does this mean that the water is pure – trout, like salmon, are known to loathe a polluted environment – but it also suggests that, with a bit of luck, this delicious and highly versatile fish might be on the menu for supper.

HISTORY

Ever since man first learned to catch trout, these fish have been invaluable as a source of food. Native Americans, ancient Britons and early Europeans all treasured these tasty fish, and it is no surprise that the fish hook was one of man's earliest tools.

Fishing rods were in use around four thousand years ago and it is known that the ancient Macedonians were adept at fly fishing for trout. They used the technique known as dapping, which involves dropping the artificial fly lightly on the surface of the water so that the fish thinks it is the real thing.

In a bid to increase the freshwater trout population, the ancient Chinese encouraged the fish to spawn on mats placed in rivers. The mats were then lifted out and the fertilized eggs were used to stock new breeding sites. The first person to artificially fertilize trout eggs is said to have been a French monk. The eggs were tightly packed in wooden boxes and buried in sand underground until they hatched.

Tickling trout

A time-honoured method for catching trout – especially popular with poachers – is tickling. This requires enormous patience as it involves sliding the hands gently under a trout that is resting under a rock, and lifting out the slippery creature before it can get away. Although the trout escapes more often than not, there are plenty of tales of individuals who perfected this practice and were rewarded with a freshly fried trout for their breakfast or dinner.

Above: Freshly caught sea trout hung up ready for cooking over an open fire.

RANGE AND HABITAT

Like salmon, to which they are related, trout are native to the northern hemisphere but they are also highly successful emigrants. Brown trout are native to Europe but they thrive in America. Conversely, the American rainbow trout has been successfully introduced to many other parts of the world. In New Zealand, for instance, the rainbow trout has acclimatized so successfully that many inhabitants of that country believe it to be one of their own native species.

LIFE CYCLE

There are many similarities between trout and salmon and both spawn in gravel pits, or redds, in fresh water. The young trout hatch after about 30 days. Initially they remain hidden in the gravel, feeding off their yolk sacs, but when this supply of food is exhausted they emerge. At this stage they are known as fry. As they grow, they develop markings, like fingerprints, on the sides of their bodies, and are described as parr, the name deriving from an Old English word for finger. Like young salmon, trout remain in their home waters for an initial period before swimming further afield to feed. Unlike salmon, however, most trout are fairly modest in their aspirations, moving to a larger river or lake rather than the ocean, although some species have adapted to living in salt water as well as fresh. Sea trout, cutthroat trout and steelhead rainbow trout are in this category. When they are several years old, the skins of these anadromous (i.e. migratory) fish become silvery and, like salmon, they are then known as smolts. They spend most of their lives at sea, returning to fresh water to spawn.

When and where individual species spawn depends on the variety of trout, the water temperature and other local conditions. Trout eggs hatch earlier than those of salmon, giving the fry time to establish themselves before their larger relatives appear on the scene.

There is considerable size variation between trout of different species and within the species themselves. The average rainbow trout on sale at the fishmonger's weighs around 350g/12oz but fishermen have reported catching fish in excess of 12kg/26lb. Sea trout that evade capture can survive for many years and grow to over 40kg/88lb, although most fish sold commercially weigh about 3kg/6½lb.

TROUT FARMING

Trout have been raised in captivity since the 1850s, initially with the aim of re-stocking freshwater rivers and lakes, but more recently for supply to the consumer. In the early years of the 20th century, a Danish trout farmer developed a system for introducing a flow of fresh water into his fish ponds to imitate river conditions. This helped reduce disease and led to improved yields. The first commercial fish farm in England was opened in 1950 and there are now more than 300 farms in the United Kingdom alone, mainly in Scotland, North Yorkshire and the south of England. As with salmon, it is very important to buy farmed trout from a responsible producer who cares for

Right: Fly fishing on the Scottish border. This method of catching trout has been popular since ancient times.

the environment as well as for his fish. Some agrochemical farmers pollute rivers with pesticides, waste fish food and sewage. The trout are packed into pens, and this makes them vulnerable to disease and infestation by fish lice.

In the wild, trout flesh is often pale pink, due to its natural diet. Some producers of farmed fish add colorants to the feed to mimic this. Organically farmed trout have creamy white flesh.

COOKING

Frying freshly caught trout over an open fire on the river bank may be the ideal, but there are many other ways of cooking this delicious fish, including poaching in court-bouillon, baking, braising, grilling (broiling) and cooking on a barbecue. Whole trout is easy to eat, as the cooked flesh falls away from the bone, but it can also be flaked and added to salads, rice or pasta dishes.

TYPES OF TROUT

There are several different types of trout. Like salmon, they all originated in the northern hemisphere, but are now widely distributed wherever appropriate water and feeding conditions exist. Although some people declare that brown trout tastes better than rainbow trout, the reality is that all types are very similar in flavour, and any variations are determined more by diet and location than variety. The texture of good quality trout is fine and firm.

Most wild trout eat a selection of plankton and small crustaceans, which gives their flesh a beautiful rose colour. In Australia, trout that feed on yabbies are particularly highly prized. Some trout farmers use carotene-rich feed so that their fish develop flesh of a similar colour to that of trout in the wild, but others, especially those who farm organically, avoid this and produce fish with creamy-coloured flesh.

Brown trout (Salmo trutta)

Also known as river or lake trout, brown trout are native to Europe, but are now widely distributed throughout the world. In appearance, brown trout vary considerably. Even in the same stretch of water, some will be a silver colour, while others will be almost black. The typical colour is brown with a red adipose (rear top) fin, yellow belly, bright red spots and a liberal sprinkling of black speckles. The flesh is very tasty, but sadly, brown trout are more often caught than bought.

Below: Sea trout

Above: Brown (right) and rainbow trout

Sea trout (Salmo trutta)

Sharp-eyed readers will have noticed that this trout has the same Latin name as brown trout. That's because scientists believe them to be the same fish, despite the differences in size and behaviour. At one time it was thought that sea trout were a separate species, because they are anadromous, like salmon, and spend most of their lives at sea, but it is now thought that they are merely a migratory form of brown trout. Sea trout are always wild, but they do not cost as much as wild salmon. They are sold whole and should be bright and silvery in colour with an almost golden sheen. The fish for sale in fishmongers and supermarkets typically weigh between 2kg/4½lb and 3kg/6½lb, with one fish enough to serve 4–6 people. Sea trout have fine, succulent, dark pink flesh and a delicate, rounded flavour.

Rainbow trout (Oncorhynchus mykiss, formerly Salmo gairdneri)

Native to North America, this highly successful fish is now found in lakes and streams in Australia, New Zealand, Central and South America, and South Africa. It is the most popular breed for fish farming. The base colour of the body is a creamy white colour, with an iridescent sheen. There is a dense black spotting on the back and sides.

Nutrition

Naturally low in sodium and calories, trout is an excellent food, especially if it is steamed, grilled or cooked in the microwave. It is high in omega-3 fatty acids, which lower blood triglycerides and reduce blood pressure, protecting the body against coronary and cardiovascular disease. Trout is also a useful source of vitamins A, B1, B2, C and D. A 100g/3½oz portion of grilled rainbow trout delivers 631kj/151kcals.

Above: Golden trout

Cutthroat trout *(Oncorhynchus clarki)*

Taking its popular name from the yellow, orange or red slash marks on either side of the lower jaw, this fish has a similar distribution to the rainbow trout, but unlike rainbow trout, most cutthroats migrate to sea when they are fully mature. Much prized by anglers, they have tasty, tender flesh, which ranges from a cream colour to deep red, depending on the local diet.

Golden trout *(Oncorhynchus mykiss aguabonita)*

This is the state fish of California. Golden trout, like coral trout, is a farmed hybrid variety, with vibrant skin and delicious red flesh that is firmer than that of its close relation, rainbow trout. The bright colouring makes both types of trout vulnerable to predators, but as farmed fish they are almost always bred and raised in a protected environment.

SMOKED TROUT

Once dismissed as poor man's smoked salmon, smoked trout is now regarded as a delicious treat in its own right. To prepare it, the fish are first brined, then cured in salt and sugar before being cold or hot smoked over oak or birch chippings. The colour ranges from rose pink to reddish brown and the best smoked trout is beautifully moist, with a more delicate flavour than that of smoked herring or mackerel. Smoked trout is usually sold as skinned fillets, but you will occasionally find them whole. Smoked trout has a wonderful flavour and tastes great with bread and butter. Horseradish cream and capers are often served as accompaniments. The fish also makes a very good pâté, or can be added to omelettes, risottos, quiches or pasta dishes. Allow one fillet per person as an appetizer; two as a main course.

Above: Smoked trout

Right: Trout roe

Left: Coral trout

TROUT ROE

Translucent orange beads of trout roe make a glorious garnish for savoury dishes. It can also be eaten in the same way as caviar, with sour cream and blinis for a delicious hors d'oeuvre to accompany a chilled glass of wine. Try the roe spread on fingers of wholemeal (whole-wheat) toast, or spooned over crème fraîche in tiny pastry cases.

BUYING AND PREPARING TROUT

Wild trout is difficult to come by, unless you happen to have a fisherman in the family. Most of the trout on sale in fish shops and supermarkets is farmed, and is likely to be rainbow trout or one of its hybrids. Brown trout is available from some specialist suppliers, and it is always worth trawling the Internet for details of organic fish farmers who will deliver your order. Make sure that the fish will be delivered within 24 hours, in an insulated container, and place a small order in the first instance so that you can satisfy yourself as to the quality of the fish and its condition on receipt.

Frozen trout is also a good buy and the fish is usually in prime condition, having been frozen so quickly that the skins still retain their natural moisture.

Sea trout is not farmed, and you will almost certainly need to order it from your fishmonger or market. This large fish has an excellent flavour and is often substituted for the more expensive salmon. Sea trout are always sold whole.

When buying fresh trout in person, the same rules apply as for any other fresh fish. Look for fish that have shiny, iridescent skins, with a good coating of slime, bright clear eyes and red gills. The skin should feel cold to the touch, and when pressed, should spring back instantly. If any indentation remains, the fish is not as fresh as it might be. Trout are almost always sold whole with the head on. They are very inexpensive.

QUANTITIES

Unless they are particularly large, you should allow one trout per person if you plan to serve it whole. A 2kg/4½lb sea trout will be sufficient to serve 4–6 people. If cooking trout fillets as part of a recipe, follow the quantity given in the instructions.

STORING AND FREEZING

When buying fresh trout, transport it in a chiller bag. Double wrap it when you get home and store it in the coldest part of the refrigerator. Aim to cook it on the same day. If this is not possible, store it for no more than two days, or freeze it. Trout freezes very well. Thaw it slowly, overnight in the refrigerator if possible.

PREPARATION

If you buy trout from a fishmonger or supermarket, it will have been cleaned, but you might be lucky enough to be offered some freshly caught trout on some occasion. In this case it is essential to know how to prepare it.

Trout do not need to be scaled, but it is a good idea to remove the fins as these can harbour bacteria. Cut them off using a strong pair of scissors. Take care with the dorsal fins (those on the back), which can have sharp spines.

CLEANING TROUT

This isn't a pleasant job, but can be performed quickly and easily with a bit of preparation. Start by spreading the work area with newspapers and topping these with greaseproof (waxed) paper.

There are two ways of gutting whole trout: through the belly or through the gills. The former is the more usual method, but gutting through the gills is preferred if splitting the fish open would spoil its appearance. This method might be used for a sea trout that was to be served whole, for instance. In either case, the gills should be removed before the fish is cooked, because they taste bitter. Do this by holding the fish on its back and opening the gill flaps. Push out the frilly gills and cut them off at the back of the head and under the jawbone with a sharp knife.

Cleaning through the belly

This is the usual way of cleaning trout. Assemble your equipment and cover the work surface before you begin.

1 Starting at the site of the anal fin, slit open the belly from tail to head, using a sharp filleting knife.

2 Pull out the innards, severing them at the throat and tail if necessary. If you are planning to stuff the trout, the roes will make a delicious addition.

3 Use a tablespoon to make sure the cavity is empty, removing any blood vessels adjacent to the backbone. Double wrap the innards and throw them away in an outside bin. Wash the cavity, then pat dry with kitchen paper.

Essential equipment
Have the necessary tools to hand before you start to prepare fish at home, as trying to work without the right equipment will make your task more difficult. Fortunately, these are not unusual or expensive items.
Chef's knife A large heavy knife is invaluable for cutting whole trout into steaks and cutlets.
Filleting knife For skinning and filleting trout, use a flexible filleting knife with a long blade. Sharpen it before you start work on the fish to make sure it cuts cleanly and evenly through fish skin and flesh.
Kitchen scissors Sharp scissors with serrated edges will make short work of removing fish fins and tails.

Cleaning through the gills

If you are planning to serve the trout whole, it is better to clean through the gills to preserve its appearance.

1 Lay the fish on its side. Make an incision in the belly, near the tail. Find the ends of the innards and snip through.

2 Cut through the bone under the lower jaw. Open the gill flaps and pull out the innards; they will come away through the flaps. Wash and dry the fish.

Filleting trout

This is a useful technique to learn if you want to cut fillets from whole trout.

1 Lay the trout on a board with its tail towards you. Lift the pectoral fin and make a diagonal cut behind the fin to the top of the head.

2 Insert the knife halfway down the body, as close to the backbone as possible. Cut towards the tail, keeping the knife flat to the bone. Lift up the released fillet, turn the knife towards the head and slide it along the bone to free the fillet completely.

3 Turn the trout over and repeat on the other side. Remove any small pin bones from the fillets with tweezers. Skin the fillets if you like.

Skinning trout fillets

1 Lay the fillet skin side down with the tail towards you. Grip the tail and angle the knife towards the skin.

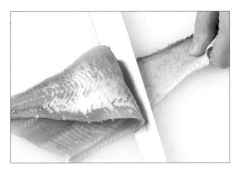

2 With a slight sawing action, cut along the length of the fillet from tail to head. Keep the skin taut.

Removing pin bones from fillets

There are always some small bones left in a fillet. Run your finger down the fillet to locate these and lift them out with tweezers.

Round fish also have tiny pin bones behind the gill fins. To remove these, make a diagonal cut on either side of the line of bones with a sharp knife. Remove the V-shaped piece of flesh together with the bones.

Boning a trout steak

Trout cutlets or bone-in steaks can be boned to give a strip of fish. This can be cooked as it is or folded back into a steak shape and tied neatly with string ready for pan-frying.

1 Insert a sharp, thin-bladed knife into the trout cutlet at the top of the bone. Cut around the bone until you reach the centre of the V-shape of the cutlet.

2 Repeat on the other side of the steak, to free the bone completely. Gently pull out the bone. Skin the fish if you want to make it more manageable.

3 Fold the skinned flesh into the middle and tie with a length of string to hold the shape.

COOKING TROUT

The secret of cooking trout successfully is the same as that for any other type of fish: less time means more taste. Undercooking can easily be remedied, but fish that is overcooked is dry and flavourless. Although the very best way to cook a fresh wild brown trout is to fry it in butter, farmed rainbow trout can be cooked in a variety of ways.

Court-bouillon

This stock, which is flavoured with white wine and aromatics, is perfect for poaching trout. Salt should be added only after cooking, as it can cause the flesh to stiffen. The recipe makes about 1 litre/1¾ pints/4 cups.

1 Slice 1 small onion, 2 carrots and the white part of 1 large leek. Put the vegetables in a pan.

2 Add 2 fresh parsley stalks, 2 bay leaves, 2 lemon slices, 300ml/½ pint/1¼ cups dry white wine and 90ml/6 tbsp white wine vinegar. Sprinkle in a few white peppercorns. Pour in 1 litre/1¾ pints/4 cups water.Bring to the boil, lower the heat and simmer for 20 minutes. Strain and leave to cool before using.

POACHING

For whole trout, you will need a fish kettle, flameproof dish or roasting pan; for smaller cuts, use an ordinary pan.

1 Remove the metal insert from the fish kettle and place the trout on this. Lower into the kettle. Add a few sprigs of fresh herbs and slices of lemon.

2 Pour cold court-bouillon, light fish stock or water over the trout in the fish kettle, adding enough of the liquid to cover the fish completely.

3 Cover the trout with buttered baking parchment. Bring the liquid slowly to simmering point. If poaching fillets, thin portions may be cooked and can be removed. Lower the heat, cover the pan and poach the uncooked thicker fillets for 5 minutes more or until done.

Fish stock

It is both easy and economical to make fish stock. For 1 litre/1¾ pints/4 cups stock you will need about 1kg/2¼lb white fish bones and trimmings from the fishmonger. Do not leave the stock simmering for too long – after 20 minutes the flavour will start to deteriorate.

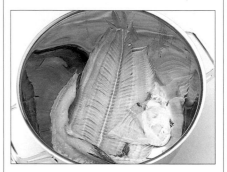

1 Wash any fish heads thoroughly and remove the gills, which would make the stock bitter. Chop the heads and bones if necessary. Put them in a large pan.

2 Slice the white part of 1 leek or ½ fennel bulb. Roughly chop 1 onion and 1 celery stick. Add to the fish heads and bones in the pan.

3 Pour in 150ml/¼ pint/⅔ cup dry white wine and 1 litre/1¾ pints/4 cups water. Add 6 whole white peppercorns and a bouquet garni. Bring to the boil.

4 Lower the heat and simmer for 20 minutes. Remove from the heat, strain through a sieve lined with muslin (cheesecloth) and cool.

COOKING "AU BLEU"

This time-honoured way of cooking trout is only for the freshest fish – so fresh that it is alive seconds before you begin the process. The term "au bleu" refers to the steely blue colour the fish skin acquires on being poached.

To cook trout "au bleu" the live fish is taken from the water and immediately stunned by a hit on the back of the head with a blunt object, such as the handle of a heavy cook's knife or a steak mallet. The fish is then cleaned through the gills and laid in a flameproof dish or fish kettle. A mixture of water and white wine vinegar is spooned over to cover it completely, and the fish is then gently simmered over a medium heat until it is cooked. A 150g/5oz trout will take 6–8 minutes, during which time the natural slime that coats the very fresh fish will turn a deep blue colour – from which the cooking method takes its name. Trout prepared in this way is traditionally served hot with hollandaise sauce, or cold with Ravigote sauce – made by mixing oil and vinegar with chopped tomatoes, diced hard-boiled eggs, capers, chopped gherkins and fresh herbs.

ROASTING

Delicate fillets of trout should be treated like white fish, such as sole or whiting, and pan-fried or steamed, but thicker trout fillets and steaks, and whole trout, can be roasted successfully. It is a good idea to marinate them in oil and lemon juice beforehand. Preheat the oven to 230°C/450°F/Gas 8 with the roasting pan inside. Add the fish, skin side down, to the pan. Fillets will take 8–10 minutes; steaks 12–15 minutes.

BAKING AND BRAISING

These are two excellent ways of cooking trout slowly, along with extra flavourings, such as fresh herbs, or vegetables.

Baking trout

Whole trout, steaks or fillets can all be baked in the oven. Slash whole fish to allow the heat to penetrate the flesh.

Lay the fish in a greased baking dish, drizzle with olive oil and add a little liquid. Dry (hard) cider goes well with trout, as do court-bouillon and fish stock. Cover with buttered baking parchment or foil and bake at no more than 200°C/400°F/Gas 6. Whole fish will cook in 20–30 minutes, depending on the thickness. Trout fillets will cook more quickly.

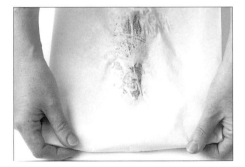

To seal in the flavour and retain moisture, bake the trout *en papillote* in a paper or foil parcel. A stuffing of rice with nuts and sun-dried tomatoes would be an excellent addition. Place the trout on a piece of oiled baking parchment or foil and fill the cavity with the stuffing. Add a drizzle of olive oil. Fold over the paper or foil to enclose the fish completely. Place the parcel on a baking sheet. Bake at 190°C/375°F/Gas 5 for about 20 minutes, until the trout is tender.

Braising trout

This is an ideal way of cooking either whole trout or fillets. Adding the stock helps to keep the fish beautifully moist.

1 Butter a flameproof dish and arrange a thick bed of thinly sliced or shredded vegetables on the base, such as a mixture of leeks, fennel and carrots.

2 Place the fish on top of the vegetables and pour on enough dry white wine, court-bouillon or light fish stock to come nearly halfway up the fish.

3 Scatter over 15ml/1 tbsp chopped fresh herbs, then cover with buttered baking parchment and set over a high heat. Bring the liquid to the boil. Braise over a low heat on top of the stove or in an oven preheated to 180°C/350°F/Gas 4 for 10–15 minutes.

FRYING

Pan-frying is a fabulously tasty way to cook trout, but stir-frying in a wok uses less oil and is a healthier alternative.

Pan-frying

Boned whole trout, steaks and fillets can be pan-fried in butter. Butter burns quite readily; adding a little oil will help prevent this. Coat the fish in seasoned flour before adding it to the melted butter, and fry over a low heat. If using whole trout, cook for 6 minutes on each side, until the skin is crisp and golden brown. After the fish has been removed from the pan, the remaining butter can be used as the basis of a sauce. Add mushrooms, a splash of pastis or ouzo and some double (heavy) cream.

Searing

Smear a frying pan with a little oil and heat until smoking. Brush both sides of the fish with oil and put into the pan skin side down. Sear for 2 minutes until the skin is golden brown, then turn the fish over and cook on the other side.

Stir-frying

Strips of trout fillet can be stir-fried in a hot wok for 1–2 minutes, but take care that they do not disintegrate. Toss the fish strips with a little sweet chilli sauce just before serving.

Deep-frying

Trout pieces are transformed into goujons by coating them in milk and flour and deep-frying in oil.

1 Dip strips of trout fillet into milk, and then into a plate of plain (all-purpose) flour that has been seasoned with salt and ground black pepper. Shake off the excess flour.

2 Heat oil for deep-frying to about 180°C/360°F or until a small cube of bread dropped into the oil turns brown in 30 seconds.

3 Lower the trout strips into the oil and fry for 3 minutes, turning with a slotted spoon, until they rise to the surface. Drain the goujons on kitchen paper and serve with a creamy dipping sauce.

GRILLING

This is one of the best ways of cooking farmed rainbow trout. If grilling (broiling) the trout whole, slash the skin on either side of the fish several times with a sharp knife. This helps to promote fast, even cooking. Marinate whole trout or steaks in a mixture of oil and lemon juice if you like, or simply brush with oil. A light dusting of ground black pepper will give the skin a delicious flavour. Place the trout in a grill (broiler) pan and cook under a medium heat for 5 minutes on each side.

MICROWAVING

Cover the fish with microwave clear film (plastic wrap) and cook on full power (100 per cent) for the time recommended in your handbook, then give it a resting period so that it finishes cooking by residual heat. As a general guide, a whole fish will take 4–7 minutes, depending on whether or not it has been stuffed. Leave to stand for a further 5 minutes before serving.

Slash whole fish several times on either side for even cooking.

Cook fillets of trout in a single layer in a microwave dish. Put thinner parts towards the centre, or tuck a thin end underneath a thicker portion.

STEAMING

As no extra fat is required and all of the nutrients are retained, this is the healthiest way to cook trout.

1 Half-fill the base pan of a steamer with water and bring to the boil. Place the trout fillets in a single layer in the steamer basket, leaving room for the steam to circulate freely.

2 Place a sheet of baking parchment over the fish, then cover the pan and steam until the fish is cooked through. Check the level of water in the steamer occasionally and top up as needed.

SMOKING

Trout can be smoked at home, either in a small domestic smoker or a kettle barbecue. Follow the instructions in your handbook. In the kitchen, the Chinese method of tea smoking works very well, but it helps if you have an extractor fan to remove the excess smoke from the kitchen.

1 Line a wok with foil and sprinkle in 30ml/2 tbsp each of raw long grain rice, sugar and aromatic tea leaves.

2 Place a wire rack on the wok and add the trout fillets in a single layer. Cover with a lid or more foil and cook over a high heat until smoke appears. Lower the heat slightly (some smoke should still escape from the wok) and cook for 6–8 minutes until the trout is done.

No steamer, no problem

If you do not possess a steamer, all is not lost. A good way to cook trout fillets over water is to place them in a single layer on a lightly buttered heatproof plate. Cover this with an inverted heatproof plate of the same size, then lift both plates together and place them over a pan of boiling water. The trout fillets will cook very quickly this way, so check them after about 3–4 minutes.

Smoked Trout Pâté

This tastes great served with crackers or spread on fingers of hot toast.

SERVES 4–6

INGREDIENTS
450g/1lb smoked trout
    fillets, skinned
1 small onion, finely chopped
1 celery stick, thinly sliced
finely grated rind and juice of
    1 lemon
200g/7oz cream cheese
salt and ground black pepper
fresh dill sprigs, to garnish

1 Tear the trout fillets into chunks and place in the bowl of a blender or food processor. Add the onion, celery and lemon rind. Scrape in the cream cheese and process until the mixture is thick and smooth.

2 Add salt and pepper to taste, then pour in just enough of the lemon juice to balance the flavours. Process briefly to mix. Serve in a small bowl, garnished with the dill.

COOK'S TIPS

• Trout is traditionally served with browned almonds, but this treatment was so widespread in the 1960s and 70s that it became somewhat passé. The flavours do complement each other, however, and recent years have seen a revival of the partnership. Also try hazelnuts, pistachios or pine nuts.
• The flavour of trout is quite robust, and responds well to warm spices like paprika, cayenne and coriander. For blackened trout, the fish are coated in melted butter, then in a mixture of garlic, onion and spices. When cooked, the spice mixture forms a dark crust – a perfect foil for the tender trout inside.
• Frozen trout must be allowed to thaw completely, and fresh trout that has been kept in the refrigerator should be brought to room temperature before cooking.
• To test whether a trout is cooked, insert a knife into the thickest part of the fish and part the flesh. It should look opaque rather than translucent and should readily separate into flakes.

EQUIPMENT

Although it is perfectly possible to prepare and cook fish without special kitchen equipment, there are a few items which make the process much easier. Some, such as the fish kettle, take up quite a lot of storage space; other gadgets, such as the fish scaler, are relatively small, but all will prove invaluable for fish cookery.

KNIVES, SCISSORS AND SCALERS

Chef's knife
A large heavy knife with a 20–25cm/8–10in blade is essential for cutting fish steaks.

Filleting knife
For filleting and skinning fish, you will need a sharp knife with a flexible blade, which is at least 15cm/6in long. This type of knife can also be used for opening shellfish. It is essential to keep a filleting knife razor sharp.

Kitchen scissors
A sturdy, sharp pair of scissors that have a serrated edge are needed for cutting off fins and trimming tails.

Fish scaler
Resembling a small grater, a fish scaler makes short work of a task that few relish.

PANS

Fish kettle
Long and deep, with rounded edges, this has handles at either end, and a tightly-fitting lid. Inside is a perforated rack or grid on which to lay the fish. This, too, has handles, and enables the cook to lift out the fish flat, without breaking it. Most modern fish kettles are made of stainless steel, but they

also come in aluminium, enamelled steel and copper with a tin-plated interior. Fish kettles are used on the hob and are invaluable for cooking whole large fish, such as salmon. Fish kettles can also be used for steaming other foods.

Oval frying pan
Such a simple idea, but intensely practical, this large pan enables you to pan-fry whole fish flat instead of bending them to fit a round pan, spoiling their shape.

Griddle pan
A ribbed cast-iron griddle pan is ideal for searing and grilling fish. They can be round, oval or rectangular. Some of the large griddles need to be used over two electric rings or gas burners on top of a stove.

Steamer
If you steam food frequently, a stainless steel steamer is a good investment. They have a lidded, deep outer pan and a perforated

inner basket. Choose a model with the widest basket you can find. Chinese bamboo steaming baskets are an economical alternative. They come in a variety of sizes, from very small dim sum baskets to very wide baskets that are about 35cm/14in across. Chinese steaming baskets can be stacked one on top of each other so that several layers of food can be cooked at one time. Cheapest of all is a small, collapsible, perforated steamer, which unfolds like a flower to fit any pan.

Below: Stainless steel steamer

Below: Chef's knife

Below: Filleting knife

Below: Scissors

Left: Chinese bamboo steamer

Left: Fish scalers

Below: Griddle pan

Above: Fish kettle

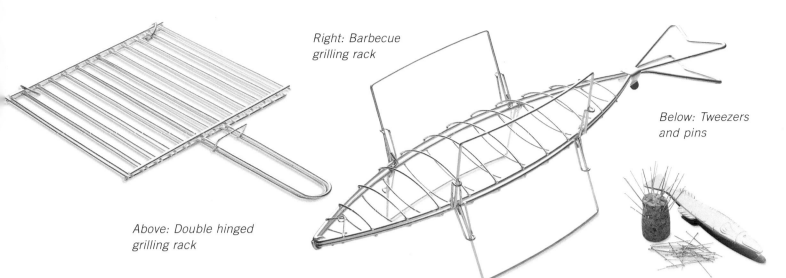

Right: Barbecue grilling rack

Below: Tweezers and pins

Above: Double hinged grilling rack

Wok

A 35cm/14in wok with a lid will be large enough to cope with most types of fish and will prove invaluable in the kitchen. There's no need to reserve this piece of equipment for stir-frying; a wok also makes an effective steamer and can also be used for deep-frying.

SPECIALIST ITEMS

Barbecue grilling racks

A hinged rack in the shape of a fish makes cooking – and turning – a single large fish relatively easy. Also very useful for general purposes is a double-sided hinged grill rack.

These can be square or rectangular and have long handles so that several fish steaks can be grilled and turned over simultaneously. However, the flat sides do tend to squash the delicate flesh of some fish. Always oil grilling racks before use to prevent the fish from sticking to them.

Fish smoker

The cheapest home-smoker is a lidded metal box with a rack to hold the fish. Smoke produced by placing dampened aromatic oak or other wood chippings, or a scattering of fresh herbs, on the coals gives extra flavour to the fish. More convenient (but more expensive) are electric fish smokers. Stove-top models can be used indoors.

OTHER USEFUL UTENSILS

Fish lifter

Resembling an elongated fish slice, the curved and perforated turner is useful for flipping over whole trout during cooking without breaking them.

Fish slice

A fish slice with a sturdy yet flexible blade will make easy work of turning whole trout, steaks and cutlets.

Pins

Use dressmakers' pins with round heads to extract tiny pin bones from trout. For safety's sake, stick them in a cork when not using.

Tweezers

Use these to extract small bones and pin bones from fish fillets.

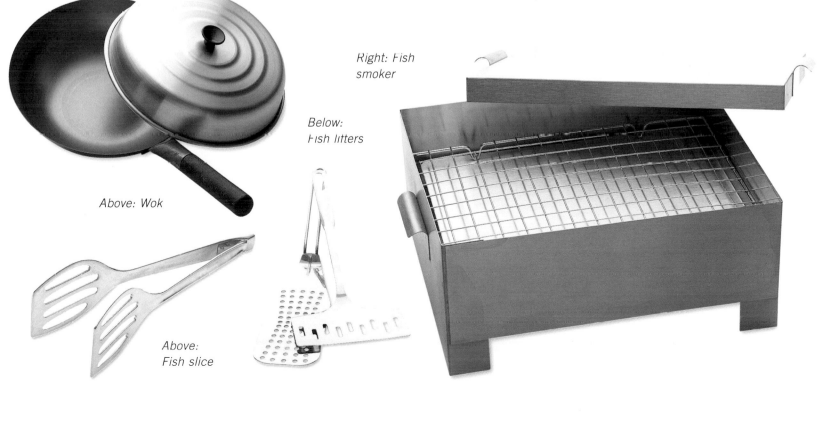

Above: Wok

Right: Fish smoker

Below: Fish lifters

Above: Fish slice

APPETIZERS
AND SNACKS

One of the many attributes of trout, aside from its excellent flavour and texture,

is the delicate pink colour, and nowhere is this capitalized on more effectively than in the

preparation of appetizers and snacks. Trout Bisque, for instance, looks so delicious in

the bowl that it would seem a shame to disturb it, were it not for the wonderful aroma

that rises from the surface. Salads, tarts, toasties and mousses are just as pretty,

especially when smoked trout is used as a wrapper, as in Three Fish Mousse.

TROUT BISQUE

A BISQUE IS A THICK, RICH, SMOOTH SOUP, USUALLY CONTAINING FISH OR SHELLFISH. THIS WONDERFULLY COLOURED PALE PINK VERSION HAS A DELICIOUSLY CREAMY TEXTURE WITH A HINT OF SPICINESS. SERVE IT WITH CRUSTY BREAD AND UNSALTED BUTTER.

SERVES 4

INGREDIENTS
    15ml/1 tbsp olive oil
    1 onion, chopped
    1 red (bell) pepper, finely chopped
    1 garlic clove, crushed
    1 medium potato, diced
    2 tomatoes, skinned and chopped
    300ml/½ pint/1¼ cups fish stock
    225g/8oz trout fillet, skinned
       and diced
    1.5ml/¼ tsp chilli powder
    15ml/1 tbsp chopped fresh
       tarragon
    300ml/½ pint/1¼ cups milk
    30ml/2 tbsp dry sherry
    150ml/¼ pint/⅔ cup double
       (heavy) cream
    salt and ground black pepper
    sprigs of watercress or rocket
       (arugula), to garnish

1 Heat the olive oil in a large pan, add the onion, pepper, garlic and potato. Fry gently for 5 minutes, stirring constantly, until the onion has just softened.

2 Add the tomatoes and stock to the pan, increase the heat and bring to the boil. Then reduce the heat and allow to simmer for 10 minutes or until the vegetables are soft.

3 Add the trout, chilli powder and chopped tarragon. Simmer gently for a further 5 minutes or until the fish is just cooked and is starting to flake when tested with a fork.

4 Remove the pan from the heat, and stir in half the milk. Set aside for 20–30 minutes to allow the contents to cool.

5 Pour the fish and vegetable mixture into a food processor and blend until smooth. Scrape into a clean pan and stir in the sherry and cream, with the remaining milk.

6 Heat the soup gently, stirring, until piping hot. Season to taste, then divide among soup bowls, garnish and serve.

COOK'S TIP
To skin the tomatoes, cut a small cross on the base of each tomato. Pour boiling water over and leave for 1 minute. The skin will then peel off very easily.

SMOKED TROUT COCOTTES

HOT SMOKED TROUT FILLETS TASTE QUITE DIFFERENT FROM COLD SMOKED TROUT; THEY HAVE A SURPRISINGLY CREAMY TEXTURE AND A WONDERFUL PALE PINK COLOUR. THIS DELICIOUS DISH MAKES A PERFECT LIGHT LUNCH FOR TWO PEOPLE, OR A FIRST COURSE FOR FOUR.

SERVES 2–4

INGREDIENTS
  4 red (bell) peppers
  60ml/4 tbsp olive oil
  150g/5oz hot smoked trout fillets
  30ml/2 tbsp chopped fresh parsley
  175g/6oz/¾ cup crème fraîche
  50g/2oz Parmesan cheese, grated
  salt and ground black pepper
  sun-dried tomato bread, to serve

1 Preheat the oven to 180°C/350°F/ Gas 4. Place the peppers in a roasting pan. Drizzle with olive oil and season well with salt and pepper. Bake for 25–30 minutes or until the pepper skins are blackened. Set aside to cool.

2 Peel the skin off the cooked peppers and discard the core and seeds. Cut the pepper flesh into bitesize pieces.

3 Preheat the oven to 200°C/400°F/ Gas 6. Flake the trout and divide between individual baking dishes. Arrange the pepper pieces in a layer over the fish in each dish.

4 Sprinkle the parsley over the fish and peppers. Spoon the crème fraîche into the dishes and season well. Top with the grated Parmesan cheese.

5 Bake in the preheated oven for about 15 minutes, or until the Parmesan cheese is golden brown and bubbling. Serve with chunks of sun-dried tomato bread, if you like.

COOK'S TIP
If making this dish for a dinner party first course, you can prepare it in advance, if you like. Keep it in the refrigerator and bake just before serving.

SEA TROUT MOUSSE

This deliciously creamy mousse makes a little sea trout go a long way. If you can't locate sea trout, it is equally good made with salmon.

SERVES 6

INGREDIENTS
  250g/9oz sea trout fillet
  120ml/4fl oz/½ cup fish stock
  2 sheets leaf gelatine, or
    15ml/1 tbsp powdered gelatine
  juice of ½ lemon
  30ml/2 tbsp dry sherry or dry vermouth
  30ml/2 tbsp freshly grated
    Parmesan cheese
  300ml/½ pint/1¼ cups whipping
    cream
  2 egg whites
  15ml/1 tbsp sunflower oil
  salt and ground white pepper

For the garnish
  5cm/2in piece cucumber, with peel,
    halved and thinly sliced
  fresh dill or chervil

COOK'S TIP
Serve the mousse with Melba toast. Toast thin slices of bread on both sides under the grill (broiler). Cut off the crusts and slice each piece of toast in half horizontally. Return to the grill pan, untoasted sides up, and toast again, taking care not to let it burn.

1 Put the sea trout in a shallow pan. Pour in the fish stock and heat to simmering point. Poach the fish for about 3–4 minutes, until it is lightly cooked. Strain the stock into a jug (pitcher) and leave the fish to cool.

2 Add the gelatine to the hot stock and stir until it has dissolved completely. Set the stock aside until required.

3 When the trout is cool enough to handle, remove the skin and flake the flesh. Pour the stock into a food processor or blender. Process briefly, then gradually add the flaked trout, lemon juice, sherry or vermouth and Parmesan through the feeder tube, continuing to process the mixture until it is smooth. Scrape into a large bowl and leave to cool completely.

4 Lightly whip the cream in a bowl; fold it into the cold trout mixture. Season to taste, then cover with clear film (plastic wrap) and chill until the mousse is just beginning to set. It should have the consistency of mayonnaise.

5 In a grease-free bowl, beat the egg whites with a pinch of salt until they form soft peaks. Using a large metal spoon, stir one-third into the trout mixture to slacken it, then fold in the rest.

6 Lightly grease six ramekins with the sunflower oil. Divide the mousse among the ramekins and level the surface. Chill in the refrigerator for 2–3 hours, until set. Just before serving, arrange a few slices of cucumber and a small herb sprig on each mousse and add a little chopped dill or chervil.

TROUT AND PRAWN POTS

BACON IS OFTEN WRAPPED AROUND WHOLE TROUT TO KEEP THE FLESH MOIST WHEN GRILLING, BUT HERE IT HAS ANOTHER FUNCTION, TO MARRY THE FLAVOURS OF TROUT AND PRAWN.

SERVES 6

INGREDIENTS
  15g/½oz/1 tbsp butter
  15ml/1 tbsp olive oil
  1 small leek, finely chopped
  2 rashers (strips) rindless back
    (lean) bacon, chopped
  115g/4oz cooked peeled prawns
    (shrimp)
  115g/4oz trout fillet, skinned
  150ml/¼ pint/⅔ cup sour cream
  1 egg, beaten
  50g/2oz Cheddar cheese, grated
  salt and ground black pepper
  warm country bread, to serve

1 Heat the butter and oil in a heavy frying pan and fry the leek gently for 5 minutes or until softened, stirring from time to time.

2 Add the bacon to the pan and fry until it is just beginning to turn colour, stirring all the time. Add the prawns, increase the heat and stir-fry the mixture for 5 minutes. Remove from the heat.

3 Cut the trout fillet into bitesize pieces and stir into the bacon and prawn mixture. Season with a little salt, if required, and plenty of pepper. Divide the mixture among six ramekins.

4 Preheat the oven to 190°C/375°F/ Gas 5. In a jug (pitcher) beat the sour cream and egg with a fork. Season lightly. Pour one-sixth of the mixture into each ramekin and sprinkle the grated cheese over the top.

5 Bake the pots in the preheated oven for 15 minutes or until the top is golden brown and bubbling. Serve straight from the oven with chunks of warm, crusty bread, if you like.

COOK'S TIPS
Trout and prawn pots can be made several hours in advance and baked just before being served for an easy, fuss-free appetizer. Store the prepared pots in the refrigerator until you are ready to cook them. If the bacon is salty, it may not be necessary to add salt to the trout mixture.

THREE FISH MOUSSE

A RICH AND CREAMY MOUSSE WHICH IS FLAVOURED WITH LEMON AND DILL — TWO OF THE CLASSIC PARTNERS FOR A WIDE RANGE OF FISH AND SHELLFISH. THIS WOULD MAKE A STUNNING FIRST COURSE, OR IT COULD BE SERVED WITH CRUSTY BREAD FOR A TASTY LUNCH.

SERVES 6–8

INGREDIENTS
15ml/1 tbsp oil
450g/1lb cod fillet, skinned
1 bay leaf
1 slice lemon
6 black peppercorns
275g/10oz thinly sliced
  smoked trout
60ml/4 tbsp cold water
15g/½oz powdered gelatine
175g/6oz cooked peeled prawns
  (shrimp), halved
300ml/½ pint/1¼ cups sour cream
225g/8oz/1 cup cream cheese
30ml/2 tbsp chopped fresh dill
juice of 1 lemon
3 drops Tabasco sauce
salt and ground black pepper
sprigs of fresh herbs, such as
  parsley or dill, and 6–8 lemon
  wedges, to garnish

VARIATION
Any firm-fleshed white fish can be substituted for the cod, including flat fish such as brill, halibut and turbot. Smoked salmon could be used instead of smoked trout.

COOK'S TIP
If you are unable to use the fish stock produced when cooking the fish in this recipe within the next 24 hours, cool it and then freeze it. Next time you make a seafood risotto or fish soup, use it as the basis of the stock.

1 Using a pastry brush, lightly brush a 1.2 litre/2 pint/5 cup ring mould with the oil. Place the cod, bay leaf, lemon and peppercorns in a pan. Cover with cold water and bring to simmering point. Poach for 10–15 minutes, or until the fish flakes when tested with a fork.

2 Meanwhile, carefully line the oiled ring mould with overlapping slices of smoked trout, leaving plenty hanging over the edge.

3 Remove the cod from the pan with a fish slice (metal spatula). Reserve the stock to use for another recipe. Chop the cod into bitesize chunks and put it in a large bowl.

4 Place the measured cold water in a small heatproof bowl and sprinkle the gelatine over the surface. Leave for 5 minutes, until spongy, then place the bowl over a pan of hot water. Stir until the gelatine has dissolved. Leave to cool slightly.

5 Add the prawns, sour cream, cream cheese and dill to the cod in the bowl. Pour in the lemon juice and Tabasco sauce. Using a fork, mash the mixture together until well combined. Season to taste with salt and plenty of ground black pepper.

6 Using a large metal spoon, fold the dissolved gelatine into the fish mixture, making sure it is evenly incorporated. Spoon into the lined ring mould and smooth down the top with the back of the spoon.

7 Lift the overhanging edges of the smoked trout and fold them over the top of the mousse. Cover the mousse with clear film (plastic wrap) and chill in the refrigerator for at least 2 hours or until set.

8 To serve, carefully run a round-bladed knife around the edge of the mousse, invert a serving plate on top and turn both over. Shake mould and plate together, if necessary, until the mousse drops out on to the plate. Garnish with the herbs and lemon wedges and serve.

TROUT AND GINGER SALAD

FRESH GRIDDLED TROUT AND SMOKED TROUT ARE DELICIOUS ON THEIR OWN. PUT THEM TOGETHER, ADD A GINGER DRESSING AND YOU HAVE A SENSATIONAL FIRST COURSE THAT IS EASY TO PREPARE.

SERVES 4

INGREDIENTS
  15ml/1 tbsp olive oil
  115g/4oz trout fillet, skinned
  grated rind and juice of ½ lime
  1 yellow (bell) pepper, finely
    chopped
  1 red (bell) pepper, finely chopped
  1 small bunch fresh coriander
    (cilantro), chopped
  115g/4oz rocket (arugula)
  115g/4oz smoked trout
  ground black pepper

For the dressing
  15ml/1 tbsp sesame oil
  75ml/5 tbsp white wine vinegar
  5ml/1 tsp soy sauce
  2.5cm/1in piece fresh root ginger,
    peeled and grated

1 Heat a griddle pan, brush it with the oil, then fry the trout fillet for 5–8 minutes, until it is just cooked. Lift the fillet out of the pan and place it in a shallow bowl. Flake the trout into bitesize pieces, sprinkle the lime rind and juice over and set aside.

COOK'S TIP
Peppery flavours go well with trout, so the rocket is an excellent choice. Buy wild rocket if possible as it has a more interesting taste. Alternatively, use watercress or even a red-leaved lettuce.
  This dish can easily be prepared in advance, but don't pour the dressing over the salad until the last minute.

2 Make the dressing by mixing the sesame oil, vinegar, soy sauce and grated root ginger in a small jug (pitcher). Whisk thoroughly until the dressing is well combined.

3 Place the chopped yellow and red peppers, coriander and rocket in a large bowl and toss to combine. Transfer the salad to a serving dish.

4 Using kitchen scissors, cut the smoked trout into bitesize pieces. Arrange the smoked trout and griddled trout fillet on the salad. Sprinkle with black pepper. Whisk the ginger dressing again and drizzle it over the salad before serving.

SPICED TROUT SALAD

MOST OF THE PREPARATION FOR THIS DELICIOUS SALAD IS DONE IN ADVANCE SO IT IS AN IDEAL DISH TO COME HOME TO AFTER A DAY ON THE BEACH OR AN AFTERNOON WALK. THE TROUT IS MARINATED IN A MIXTURE OF CORIANDER, GINGER AND CHILLI AND SERVED WITH COLD BABY ROAST POTATOES.

SERVES 4

INGREDIENTS

  2.5cm/1in piece fresh root ginger,
    peeled and finely grated
  1 garlic clove, crushed
  5ml/1 tsp hot chilli powder
  15ml/1 tbsp coriander seeds,
    lightly crushed
  grated rind and juice of 2 lemons
  60ml/4 tbsp olive oil
  450g/1lb trout fillet, skinned
  900g/2lb new potatoes
  5–10ml/1–2 tsp sea salt
  ground black pepper
  15ml/1 tbsp whole or chopped fresh
    chives, to garnish

1 Mix the ginger, garlic, chilli powder, coriander seeds and lemon rind in a bowl. Whisk in the lemon juice with 15ml/1 tbsp of the olive oil to make a marinade.

2 Place the trout in a shallow, non-metallic dish and cover with the marinade. Turn the fish to make sure they are well coated, cover with clear film (plastic wrap) and chill for at least 2 hours or overnight.

COOK'S TIP
Look for firm pieces of fresh root ginger, with smooth skin. If bought really fresh, root ginger will keep for up to two weeks in a cool, dry place, away from strong light. Root ginger freezes successfully and can be shaved or grated straight from the freezer.

3 Preheat the oven to 200°C/400°F/ Gas 6. Place the potatoes in a roasting pan, toss them in 30ml/2 tbsp olive oil and season with salt and pepper. Roast for 45 minutes or until tender. Remove from the oven and set aside to cool.

4 Reduce the oven temperature to 190°C/375°F/Gas 5. Remove the trout from the marinade and place in a roasting pan. Bake for 20 minutes or until cooked through. Remove from the oven and leave to cool.

5 Cut the potatoes into chunks, flake the trout into bitesize pieces and toss them together in a serving dish with the remaining olive oil. Sprinkle with the chives and serve.

VARIATION
If you don't like spicy hot food, omit the chilli powder in the marinade – the trout tastes equally good without it.

SMOKED TROUT SALAD

HORSERADISH IS AS GOOD A PARTNER TO SMOKED TROUT AS IT IS TO ROAST BEEF. IN THIS RECIPE IT IS MIXED WITH YOGURT, MUSTARD POWDER, OIL AND VINEGAR TO MAKE A DELICIOUSLY PIQUANT LIGHT SALAD DRESSING THAT COMPLEMENTS THE SMOKED TROUT PERFECTLY.

SERVES 4

INGREDIENTS
  1 oakleaf or other red lettuce
  225g/8oz small tomatoes, cut into
    thin wedges
  ½ cucumber, peeled and thinly
    sliced
  4 smoked trout fillets, each about
    200g/7oz, skinned and flaked

For the dressing
  pinch of mustard powder
  15–20ml/3 4 tsp white wine vinegar
  30ml/2 tbsp light olive oil
  100ml/3½fl oz/scant ½ cup natural
    (plain) yogurt
  about 30ml/2 tbsp grated fresh or
    bottled horseradish
  pinch of caster (superfine) sugar

1 Make the dressing. Mix the mustard powder and white wine vinegar in a bowl, then gradually whisk in the olive oil, yogurt, horseradish and sugar. Set aside for 30 minutes to allow all the flavours to develop.

COOK'S TIP
Fresh grated horseradish varies in potency. If it is very strong, whisk only half the suggested amount into the dressing. If the only horseradish you can find is the creamed variety, you can still use it in the recipe, but mix it with the yogurt first.

2 Place the lettuce leaves in a large bowl. Stir the dressing again, then pour half of it over the leaves and toss them lightly using two wooden spoons.

3 Arrange the lettuce on four individual plates with the tomatoes, cucumber and trout. Spoon over the remaining dressing and serve immediately.

SMOKED TROUT TARTLETS

CRISP, GOLDEN FILO PASTRY CONTRASTS WITH A CREAMY TROUT AND THREE-CHEESE FILLING IN THESE PRETTY LITTLE TARTLETS.

SERVES 4

INGREDIENTS
  8 x 15cm/6in squares filo pastry
  50g/2oz/¼ cup butter, melted
  50g/2oz Gruyère cheese, grated
  115g/4oz/½ cup mascarpone cheese
  50g/2oz Parmesan cheese, grated
  45ml/3 tbsp milk
  75g/3oz smoked trout
  8 cherry tomatoes, halved
  salt and ground black pepper
  fresh flat leaf parsley and salad
    leaves, to garnish

3 In a large bowl, combine the three cheeses and milk. Season generously with salt and pepper and mix well.

1 Preheat the oven to 180°C/350°F/ Gas 4. For each tartlet, place two squares of filo pastry on top of each other at angles to form a star shape. Brush with melted butter and place, buttered side down, in an individual Yorkshire pudding pan or 10cm/4in tartlet pan. Repeat with the remaining filo.

2 Support the pans on a baking sheet and brush the pastry with a little more butter. Bake for 5 minutes or until the tartlets are crisp and light golden brown in colour. Remove the tartlets from the oven but leave the oven on.

4 Cut the smoked trout into bitesize pieces using kitchen scissors or a knife. Arrange the halved tomatoes and trout in the pastry cases.

5 Spoon the cheese mixture into the cooked pastry cases, gently pressing it down with the back of a spoon. Return the tartlets to the oven and bake for 10–15 minutes more, until the cheese is bubbling and golden brown. Serve immediately on individual plates, garnished with the parsley and a few salad leaves.

COOK'S TIPS
• Cover the filo pastry sheets with a damp, clean dishtowel or clear film (plastic wrap) until you are ready to use them, so that they do not dry out.
• Although Gruyère is the preferred cheese for these tartlets, Emmenthal or Jarlsberg could be used instead. Grate the cheese finely with a microplane grater.

SEARED TROUT BRUSCHETTA

THESE RESEMBLE OPEN SANDWICHES AND ARE HEARTY ENOUGH TO MAKE A SATISFYING LUNCHTIME SNACK FOR FOUR PEOPLE. IF YOU PREFER, CUT THE LOAF INTO EIGHT AND SERVE AS AN APPETIZER.

SERVES 4–8

INGREDIENTS
    1 baguette
    1 garlic clove, halved
    30ml/2 tbsp extra virgin olive oil
    120ml/4fl oz/½ cup crème fraîche or
        sour cream
    15ml/1 tbsp creamed horseradish
    15ml/1 tbsp chopped fresh chives
    4 thin trout fillets, each about
        115g/4oz
    50g/2oz watercress, land cress or
        salad leaves
    salt and ground black pepper
    lemon juice and extra virgin olive oil,
        to serve

1 Preheat the grill (broiler) to high and preheat the oven to 150°C/300°F/Gas 2. Cut the baguette in half horizontally, then cut each half vertically to give four equal-sized pieces altogether.

2 Toast the bread under the grill until lightly browned. Rub the toasted bread all over with the halved garlic clove and drizzle with olive oil. Keep warm in the oven while you prepare the topping.

3 In a small bowl, mix the crème fraîche or sour cream, horseradish and chives with salt and pepper to taste.

4 Season the trout fillets lightly and brush over a little olive oil. Heat a frying pan until really hot and add the trout, placing the fillets skin side down. Sear for 3 minutes, flip over and cook for 30 seconds more.

5 Place one seared trout fillet on each piece of toasted baguette. Add a generous dollop of the horseradish cream and some watercress, land cress or salad leaves. Serve drizzled with lemon juice and extra olive oil.

VARIATIONS
• If you prefer, use 15ml/1 tbsp wholegrain mustard instead of the horseradish in the creamy filling, and substitute chopped fresh flat leaf parsley for the chives.
• Try extra virgin olive oil flavoured with herbs, such as thyme and rosemary, for drizzling over the toasted bread.

HOT TROUT WITH RED VEGETABLES

THIS MEDITERRANEAN-STYLE SANDWICH IS SO EASY TO PREPARE AND MAKES A TASTY WEEKEND LUNCH.
CHOOSE YOUR FAVOURITE BREAD, BUT MAKE SURE IT IS REALLY FRESH.

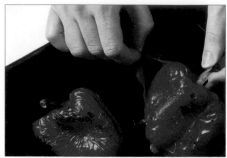

3 Peel the skin off the cooked peppers and discard the core and seeds. Cut the pepper flesh into strips. Slice each ciabatta loaf in half vertically, then cut each half in half horizontally.

4 Heat a ridged griddle pan over a medium heat. Lift the trout fillets carefully out of the marinade and fry them for 1–2 minutes, without adding any oil, until just cooked.

5 Mix the pesto and mayonnaise together and spread over the bread. Divide the rocket among four halves of the bread and top with the trout fillet, pepper strips and roasted tomatoes. Place the remaining bread on top and serve.

COOK'S TIPS
• You can use any bread you like but make sure you slice the bread thickly.
• Small loaves of olive-oil bread, such as ciabatta and focaccia, are ideal for these sandwiches. Try the sun-dried tomato and black olive versions, too.
• If you can't find any red pesto, use 30ml/2 tbsp chopped fresh basil mixed with 15ml/1 tbsp sun-dried tomato paste.

SERVES 4

INGREDIENTS
  2 red (bell) peppers
  8 cherry tomatoes
  60ml/4 tbsp extra virgin olive oil
  30ml/2 tbsp lemon juice
  4 thin trout fillets, each about
    115g/4oz, skinned
  2 small ciabatta loaves
  15ml/1 tbsp red pesto
  30ml/2 tbsp mayonnaise
  115g/4oz rocket (arugula)
  salt and ground black pepper

1 Preheat the oven to 180°C/350°F/ Gas 4. Place the peppers and tomatoes in a roasting pan and drizzle half the olive oil over. Bake for 25–30 minutes or until the pepper skins are blackened. Set aside to cool.

2 In a small bowl or jug (pitcher), whisk the remaining oil with the lemon juice and a little salt and freshly ground black pepper. Place the trout in a shallow, non-metallic dish and pour over the oil and lemon juice. Turn the fish to make sure they are well coated.

GOAT'S CHEESE AND TROUT TOASTIES

THESE LITTLE ROUNDS ARE PACKED FULL OF FLAVOUR — THE GOAT'S CHEESE AND TROUT COMBINE BEAUTIFULLY TO MAKE A DELICIOUS SNACK SUITABLE FOR ANY TIME OF THE DAY.

SERVES 4

INGREDIENTS

  8 thick slices of white bread
  30ml/2 tbsp olive oil
  5ml/1 tsp fresh thyme leaves
  20ml/4 tsp pesto
  50g/2oz smoked trout slices
  4 round goat's cheese slices,
    each about 50g/2oz
  salt and ground black pepper
  cherry tomatoes and fresh basil,
    to serve

COOK'S TIP
The easiest way to crumb a small quantity of bread is with a hand-held grater. Rub the bread down the coarsest side, in the same way as grating cheese. Fresh breadcrumbs can be stored in the freezer until you need them.

1 Preheat the oven to 200°C/400°F/ Gas 6. Using a pastry cutter that is slightly larger than the goat's cheese rounds, cut a circle from each slice of bread.

2 Brush the bread rounds with a little olive oil, scatter with a few thyme leaves and season well. Place the bread rounds on a baking sheet and bake for 5 minutes or until crisp and a light golden colour.

3 Remove the bread from the oven and spread 5ml/1 tsp pesto over half the rounds. Divide the smoked trout among the pesto-topped bread, top with the cheese rounds and season well with black pepper. Top the cheese with the remaining bread circles.

4 Bake the toasties in the oven for 5 minutes more, until the cheese has just started to soften slightly. Remove from the oven and serve immediately with the cherry tomatoes and basil leaves.

VARIATIONS
• Thyme goes particularly well with goat's cheese but other strong herbs can be substituted. Try oregano, marjoram or sage for a completely different taste.
• For a milder flavour, use rounds of under-ripe Brie or Camembert cheese in place of the goat's cheese.

CHEESE SCONES WITH TROUT BUTTER

THESE DELICIOUS SCONES ARE TOPPED WITH A RICHLY FLAVOURED SMOKED TROUT AND HORSERADISH BUTTER, WHICH CAN BE PREPARED A DAY AHEAD. THE CHEESE SCONES ARE BEST BAKED ON THE DAY YOU ARE PLANNING TO EAT THEM AS THEY STALE QUITE QUICKLY.

MAKES 6

INGREDIENTS
75g/3oz/¾ cup self-raising
  (self-rising) flour
75g/3oz/¾ cup plain (all-purpose)
  flour
5ml/1 tsp baking powder
25g/1oz/2 tbsp butter
75g/3oz Cheddar cheese or
  Monterey Jack, grated
1 egg, beaten
45ml/3 tbsp milk
salt and ground black pepper
fresh parsley sprigs, to garnish

For the butter
50g/2oz/¼ cup butter, softened
50g/2oz smoked trout
5ml/1 tsp creamed horseradish

COOK'S TIP
For the lightest scones, handle the dough as little as possible, mixing the ingredients together quickly and kneading the dough as briefly as possible. Sifting the flours into the mixing bowl from a height will help to incorporate additional air into the scone mixture.

VARIATIONS
Other hard cheeses, such as Red Leicester or Lancashire, could be used instead of the Cheddar or Monterey Jack for the cheese scones.

1 Make the smoked trout butter. Place the softened butter, smoked trout and creamed horseradish in a food processor. Season to taste with salt and ground black pepper. Process the ingredients until well blended. Transfer to a bowl, cover and chill until needed.

2 Preheat the oven to 220°C/425°F/ Gas 7. To make the scones, sift the flours and baking powder into a mixing bowl. Season the flour with salt and ground black pepper.

3 Rub the butter into the flour with your fingertips until the mixture resembles fine breadcrumbs. Stir in most of the cheese, reserving just enough to sprinkle on top of the scones.

4 Stir in the beaten egg and enough milk to make a smooth, soft dough. Knead the dough gently and turn it out on a floured surface. Roll or pat the dough out to a thickness of 2cm/¾in. Using a plain 7.5cm/3in cutter, stamp out six scones.

5 Place the scones on a well-greased baking sheet, brush with a little milk to glaze and sprinkle the reserved cheese over. Bake for 15–20 minutes or until just turning golden. Cool slightly on a wire rack.

6 Remove the smoked trout butter from the refrigerator 30 minutes before serving. Split the warm scones in half, top with the butter and garnish with the parsley to serve.

SMOKED TROUT SOUFFLÉ OMELETTE

HALF OMELETTE, HALF SOUFFLÉ, THIS DELICIOUSLY LIGHT SUPPER DISH IS THE IDEAL CHOICE FOR WHEN YOU'RE JUST COOKING FOR YOURSELF. PACKED WITH FRESH HERBS AND SMOKED TROUT, IT IS FULL OF FLAVOUR. SERVE IT SIMPLY WITH A GLASS OF DRY WHITE WINE, SOME WARM COUNTRY BREAD AND A FRESH SALAD SUCH AS BASIL AND TOMATO.

SERVES 1

INGREDIENTS

2 eggs, separated
30ml/2 tbsp water
25g/1oz/2 tbsp butter
15ml/1 tbsp chopped fresh parsley
15ml/1 tbsp chopped fresh chives
50g/2oz smoked trout, roughly
  chopped
40g/1½oz Gruyère cheese,
  finely grated
salt and ground black pepper
warm bread, to serve

For the tomato and basil salad
3 plum tomatoes, sliced
30ml/2 tbsp fresh basil leaves
5ml/1 tsp balsamic vinegar
15ml/1 tbsp extra virgin olive oil

COOK'S TIP
For the best results when whisking, the egg whites should be at room temperature. If you store eggs in the refrigerator, remember to take them out 30 minutes or so before you want to use them.

VARIATIONS
• Any fresh herbs, such as chervil, oregano or thyme – or a mixture of all of them – can be substituted for the chives and parsley in this recipe.
• Instead of Gruyère cheese, try another full-flavoured hard cheese, such as Cheddar or Monterey Jack.

1 Make the salad. Arrange the tomato slices on a serving plate and top with the fresh basil leaves. Drizzle the vinegar and oil over and season well. Set aside but do not chill, as the sweet flavour of the tomatoes will be more pronounced at room temperature.

2 Put the egg whites in a mixing bowl and add salt and pepper. Using a hand-held electric mixer or rotary whisk, whisk until they are stiff but not dry. In a separate mixing bowl, whisk the egg yolks with the water until creamy.

3 Using a large metal spoon, add a little of the egg white mixture to the yolks. Fold in carefully to incorporate as much air as possible. Add the remaining white and fold in gently.

4 Preheat the grill (broiler) to high. Melt the butter in an 18cm/7in omelette or frying pan which can safely be used under the grill. Swirl the pan around to grease the sides thoroughly.

5 Pour the egg mixture into the pan and cook over a medium heat, gently shivering the pan from time to time, until the omelette is golden brown on the base and just firm to the touch in the centre.

6 Sprinkle over the chopped herbs, smoked trout and grated cheese.

7 Place the pan under the grill and cook until the egg is just set and the cheese is golden and bubbling. Run a blunt knife around the edge of the pan to release the omelette, then gently score a line right across the centre of the omelette.

8 Fold the omelette in half and slide it carefully on to a hot serving plate. Serve immediately with the tomato and basil salad and warm bread.

BAKED TROUT WITH A GREMOLATA CRUST

A GREMOLATA CRUST IS A COMBINATION OF BREADCRUMBS WITH FINELY CHOPPED PARSLEY, LEMON RIND AND GARLIC. IT IS TRADITIONALLY SPRINKLED OVER THE CLASSIC VEAL DISH, OSSO BUCCO.

SERVES 4

INGREDIENTS

1 small aubergine (eggplant),
  cubed
1 red (bell) pepper, finely
  diced
1 yellow (bell) pepper, finely
  diced
1 small red onion, finely chopped
30ml/2 tbsp olive oil
350g/12oz trout fillets
juice of 1 lime
salt and ground black pepper
chunks of bread, to serve

For the gremolata crust
  grated rind of 1 lemon
  grated rind of 1 lime
  25g/1oz/½ cup fresh breadcrumbs
  30ml/2 tbsp chopped fresh flat
    leaf parsley
  1 garlic clove, finely chopped

1 Preheat the oven to 200°C/400°F/ Gas 6. Place the aubergine, peppers and onion in a roasting pan. Add the oil and stir to coat all the vegetables. Sprinkle with plenty of salt and pepper. Cook for 40 minutes or until the edges of the vegetables have begun to char.

2 Make the gremolata by mixing the lemon and lime rind with the breadcrumbs, chopped parsley and garlic. Add plenty of salt and pepper.

3 Place the trout fillets on top of the vegetables in the roasting pan and cover the surface of the fish with the breadcrumb mixture. Return to the oven for a further 15 minutes or until the fish is fully cooked and the gremolata topping is crunchy.

4 Divide the fish and vegetables among four serving plates and sprinkle the lime juice over to taste. Serve with bread to soak up all the juices.

TROUT-FILLED PITTAS WITH MUSTARD MAYO

MUSTARD AND TROUT MAY NOT BE AN OBVIOUS COMBINATION OF FLAVOURS, BUT THEY TASTE GREAT WHEN TEAMED TOGETHER IN THESE SIMPLE FILLED PITTA BREADS.

SERVES 4

INGREDIENTS

175g/6oz hot smoked trout fillets
6 sun-dried tomatoes in oil, drained
  and finely chopped
90ml/6 tbsp mayonnaise
10ml/2 tsp wholegrain mustard
4 pitta breads
2 Little Gem (Bibb) lettuces
1 yellow (bell) pepper, finely diced
salt and ground black pepper

COOK'S TIP
The pitta breads can be warmed in
a toaster if you prefer. Watch them
carefully so that they do not burn.
They are ready as soon as they start
to puff up.

1 Preheat the oven to 180°C/350°F/
Gas 4. To make the filling, flake the
trout into small pieces and place in
a large mixing bowl.

2 Add the chopped sun-dried tomatoes,
mayonnaise and mustard to the trout
in the bowl. Season to taste with salt
and plenty of ground black pepper.
Stir well to combine all the ingredients.

3 Wrap the pitta breads in foil and heat
them in the oven for 10 minutes.

4 Chop or shred the lettuces and mix
with the yellow pepper in a bowl.

5 Remove the pitta breads from the
oven and split each one along one side
with a sharp knife. Half fill each pitta
with the lettuce and pepper mixture.
Add one quarter of the trout mixture
and season well before serving.

MAIN MEALS

We should be eating oily fish like trout at least two or three times a week, but although many of us intend to do just that, we sometimes get stuck in a recipe rut. If you've ever found yourself running out of ideas, you certainly won't once you've tried the delicious new recipes in this chapter. Dishes like Pan-fried Citrus Trout with Basil, Trout Gougère and Trout and Asparagus Pie are easy to prepare and taste great. Also on the menu are old favourites like Trout with Almonds and Trout with Tarragon Sauce.

CHINESE-STYLE STEAMED TROUT

*IF YOU THINK STEAMED TROUT SOUNDS DULL, THINK AGAIN. THIS FISH, MARINATED IN A BLACK BEAN,
GINGER AND GARLIC MIXTURE BEFORE BEING MOISTENED WITH RICE WINE AND SOY SAUCE, IS SUPERB.*

3 Place a little ginger and garlic inside the cavity of each fish, then lay them on a plate or dish that will fit inside a large steamer. Rub the bean mixture into the fish, working it into the slashes, then sprinkle the remaining ginger and garlic over the top. Cover with clear film (plastic wrap) and place the fish in the refrigerator for at least 30 minutes.

4 Remove the fish from the refrigerator and place the steamer over a pan of boiling water. Sprinkle the rice wine or sherry and half the soy sauce over the fish and place the plate of fish inside the steamer. Steam for 15–20 minutes, or until the fish is cooked and the flesh flakes easily when tested with a fork.

SERVES 6

INGREDIENTS
  2 trout, each about 675–800g/
    1½–1¾lb
  25ml/1½ tbsp salted black beans
  2.5ml/½ tsp granulated sugar
  30ml/2 tbsp finely shredded fresh
    root ginger
  4 garlic cloves, thinly sliced
  30ml/2 tbsp Chinese rice wine or
    dry sherry
  30ml/2 tbsp light soy sauce
  4–6 spring onions (scallions), finely
    shredded or sliced diagonally
  45ml/3 tbsp groundnut (peanut) oil
  10ml/2 tsp sesame oil

1 Wash the fish inside and out under cold running water, then pat dry on kitchen paper. Using a sharp knife, slash 3–4 deep crosses on either side of each fish.

2 Place half the black beans and the sugar in a small bowl and mash together with the back of a fork. When the beans are thoroughly mashed, stir in the remaining whole beans.

5 Using a fish slice (metal spatula), carefully lift the fish on to a warmed serving dish. Sprinkle the fish with the remaining soy sauce, then sprinkle with the shredded or sliced spring onions.

6 In a small pan, heat the groundnut oil until very hot and smoking, then trickle it over the spring onions and fish. Lightly sprinkle the sesame oil over the fish and serve immediately.

TROUT WITH SPINACH AND MUSHROOM SAUCE

SKINNED TROUT FILLETS ARE THE LAZY COOK'S IDEAL INGREDIENT. THEY COOK QUICKLY AND TASTE DELICIOUS, ESPECIALLY WHEN SERVED WITH A RICH SPINACH AND MUSHROOM SAUCE.

SERVES 4

INGREDIENTS

75g/3oz/6 tbsp unsalted
  (sweet) butter
¼ medium onion, chopped
225g/8oz/3 cups field
  (portabello) mushrooms,
  chopped
300ml/½ pint/1¼ cups boiling
  chicken stock
225g/8oz frozen chopped spinach
10ml/2 tsp cornflour (cornstarch)
15ml/1 tbsp water
150ml/¼ pint/⅔ cup crème fraîche
  or sour cream
8 trout fillets, skinned
a pinch of freshly grated nutmeg
salt and ground black pepper
new potatoes, baby carrots and
  baby corn cobs, to serve

3 Mix the cornflour to a paste with the water. Stir into the mushroom mixture. Simmer gently, stirring often, until the sauce thickens.

4 Scrape the sauce into a blender or food processor and process until smooth. Add the crème fraîche or sour cream, nutmeg, salt and pepper. Pour into a serving sauceboat and keep warm.

5 Melt the remaining butter in a large frying pan. Season the trout fillets with salt and ground black pepper and cook for 6 minutes, turning once, until just cooked through. Serve with new potatoes, baby carrots and baby corn cobs. The sauce can be poured over the trout fillets or served separately.

1 To make the sauce, melt 50g/2oz/¼ cup of the butter in a frying pan or wok and fry the onion until soft. Add the mushrooms and cook until the juices begin to run, stirring occasionally with a wooden spoon.

2 Pour the hot stock into the pan, then stir in the frozen spinach and cook, stirring from time to time, until the spinach has thawed completely.

COOK'S TIP

A hand-held electric blender is ideal for processing the spinach and mushroom sauce. If you process the sauce in the pan, you can leave it there to keep warm until you are ready to serve it.

PAN-FRIED CITRUS TROUT <u>WITH</u> BASIL

THE CLEAN TASTE OF ORANGES AND LEMONS AND THE AROMATIC SCENT OF BASIL COMBINE
BEAUTIFULLY IN THIS RECIPE TO CREATE A LIGHT AND TANGY SAUCE FOR TROUT FILLETS.

<u>SERVES 4</u>

INGREDIENTS

4 trout fillets, each about 200g/7oz
2 lemons
3 oranges
105ml/7 tbsp olive oil
45ml/3 tbsp plain (all-purpose)
  flour
25g/1oz/2 tbsp butter
5ml/1 tsp soft light brown sugar
15g/½ oz/½ cup fresh basil leaves
salt and ground black pepper

1 Arrange the trout fillets in the base of a non-metallic shallow dish. Grate the rind from one lemon and two of the oranges, then squeeze these fruits and pour the combined juices into a jug (pitcher). Slice the remaining fruits and reserve to use as a garnish.

2 Add 75ml/5 tbsp of the oil to the citrus juices. Beat with a fork and pour over the fish. Cover and leave to marinate in the refrigerator for at least 2 hours.

3 Preheat the oven to 150°C/300°F/ Gas 2. Using a fish slice or metal spatula, carefully remove the trout from the marinade. Season the fish and coat each in flour.

4 Heat the remaining oil in a frying pan and add the fish. Fry for 2–3 minutes on each side until cooked, then transfer to a plate and keep hot in the oven.

5 Add the butter and the marinade to the pan and heat gently, stirring until the butter has melted. Season with salt and pepper, then stir in the sugar. Continue cooking gently for 4–5 minutes until the sauce has thickened slightly.

6 Finely shred half the basil leaves and add them to the pan. Pour the sauce over the fish and garnish with the remaining basil and the orange and lemon slices.

COOK'S TIP
Basil leaves bruise easily, so they should always be shredded by hand or used whole rather than cut with a knife.

TROUT <u>AND</u> SOLE PARCELS <u>WITH</u> VERMOUTH

TWO TYPES OF FISH, BOTH DELICATE BUT WITH DIFFERENT FLAVOURS, MAKE A WONDERFUL DISH WHEN SANDWICHED WITH A WATERCRESS FILLING AND SERVED WITH A SAUCE SPIKED WITH VERMOUTH.

SERVES 4

INGREDIENTS

1 bunch watercress or rocket (arugula)
1 courgette (zucchini), grated
5ml/1 tsp Tabasco sauce
grated rind and juice of 1 lemon
450g/1lb trout fillets, skinned
450g/1lb sole fillets, skinned
50g/2oz/¼ cup butter
150ml/¼ pint/⅔ cup fish stock
120ml/4fl oz/½ cup dry white
  vermouth
salt and ground black pepper
watercress or rocket (arugula) sprigs,
  to garnish

1 Preheat the oven to 200°C/400°F/ Gas 6. Strip the watercress or rocket leaves from the stalks and chop them finely. Place them in a bowl with the grated courgette, Tabasco sauce, lemon rind and juice. Season with salt and pepper to taste.

2 Season the trout and sole fillets on both sides with salt and pepper. Cover each sole fillet in turn with the watercress or rocket mixture. Top with the trout fillets.

3 Tie the fish "sandwiches" into neat parcels with raffia or string (twine). Arrange the fish parcels side by side in a shallow flameproof dish and dot all over with the butter.

4 Pour the stock and vermouth over, cover and bake for 20 minutes until the fish is tender. Carefully lift the fish parcels on to a serving platter and keep them hot.

5 Transfer the flameproof dish to the top of the stove and cook the stock mixture until it has reduced by half. Pour the sauce over the fish, garnish with watercress or rocket and serve.

COOK'S TIP
If the fish fillets are of uneven sizes, trim the larger piece. Finely chop the trimmings and add to the stuffing.

TROUT <u>WITH</u> TAMARIND <u>AND</u> CHILLI SAUCE

TROUT IS A VERY ECONOMICAL FISH, BUT CAN TASTE A BIT BLAND. THIS SPICY THAI-INSPIRED SAUCE REALLY GIVES IT A ZING. IF YOU LIKE YOUR FOOD VERY SPICY, ADD AN EXTRA CHILLI.

SERVES 4

INGREDIENTS
   4 trout, about 350g/12oz each,
     cleaned
   6 spring onions (scallions), sliced
   60ml/4 tbsp soy sauce
   15ml/1 tbsp groundnut (peanut) oil
   30ml/2 tbsp chopped fresh
     coriander (cilantro)

For the sauce
   50g/2oz tamarind pulp
   105ml/7 tbsp boiling water
   2 shallots, roughly chopped
   1 fresh red chilli, seeded and chopped
   1cm/½in piece fresh root ginger,
     peeled and chopped
   5ml/1 tsp soft brown sugar
   45ml/3 tbsp Thai fish sauce

1 Slash each trout diagonally four or five times on either side with a sharp knife. Place in one or two shallow dishes.

2 Fill the cavities with spring onions. Douse each fish on both sides with soy sauce, turning the fish over carefully. Sprinkle on any remaining spring onions and set aside until required.

3 Make the sauce. Put the tamarind pulp in a small bowl and pour on the boiling water. Mash with a fork until soft. Tip into a food processor or blender and add the shallots, fresh chilli, ginger, sugar and fish sauce. Whizz to a coarse pulp.

4 Heat the oil in a large frying pan or wok and fry the trout, one at a time if necessary, for about 5 minutes on each side, until the skin is crisp and browned and the flesh cooked. Put on warmed plates and spoon over some sauce. Sprinkle with the coriander and serve.

TROUT WITH ALMONDS

SOME PEOPLE REGARD THIS DISH AS A CLICHÉ, BUT IF THAT'S TRUE, IT'S A CLICHÉ THAT HAS ENDURED FOR A LONG TIME. THE REASON IS SIMPLE: THIS COMBINATION WORKS EXTREMELY WELL.

SERVES 2

INGREDIENTS

2 trout, each about 350g/12oz, cleaned
40g/1½oz/⅓ cup plain (all-purpose) flour
50g/2oz/¼ cup butter
25g/1oz/¼ cup flaked (sliced) almonds
30ml/2 tbsp dry white wine
salt and ground black pepper
new potatoes and mixed green salad, to serve

3 Add the remaining butter to the pan and cook the almonds, shaking the pan frequently, until just lightly browned.

4 Add the white wine to the pan and boil for 1 minute, stirring constantly, until the sauce is slightly syrupy. Pour or spoon the sauce and almonds over each fish and serve immediately with boiled new potatoes and a green salad.

VARIATION
Other nuts can be used instead of almonds. Hazelnuts are particularly good with trout. The nuts swiftly brown and go crisp, so watch them closely to prevent them burning.

1 Rinse the trout and pat dry. Put the flour in a large plastic bag and season with salt and pepper. Place the trout, one at a time, in the bag and shake to coat with flour. Shake off the excess flour from the fish and discard the remaining flour.

2 Melt half the butter in a large frying pan over a medium heat. When it is foamy, add the trout and cook for 6–7 minutes on each side, until the skin is golden brown and the flesh next to the bone is opaque. Transfer the fish to warmed plates and cover to keep warm.

TROUT <u>WITH</u> CUCUMBER CREAM

CREAM SAUCES SUIT THE DELICATE FLAVOUR OF TROUT VERY WELL.
THIS ONE INTRODUCES TWO MORE COMPLEMENTARY ELEMENTS,
CUCUMBER AND TARRAGON.

SERVES 4

INGREDIENTS
  25g/1oz/2 tbsp butter
  8 fresh trout fillets, skinned
  2 large spring onions (scallions),
    white parts only, chopped
  ½ cucumber, peeled, seeded and
    cut into short batons
  5ml/1 tsp cornflour (cornstarch)
  150ml/¼ pint/⅔ cup single
    (light) cream
  50ml/2fl oz/¼ cup dry sherry
  30ml/2 tbsp chopped fresh tarragon
  1 tomato, halved, seeded and
    chopped
  salt and ground black pepper
  new potatoes and green beans,
    to serve

1 Melt the butter in a large frying pan. Season the trout fillets and cook for 6 minutes, turning once. Transfer to a warm plate, cover and keep hot.

2 Add the spring onions and cucumber to the butter remaining in the pan. Cook over a gentle heat, stirring, until soft but not coloured.

3 Put the cornflour (cornstarch) in a cup and stir in about 30ml/2 tbsp of the cream to make a thin paste.

4 Add the remaining cream to the pan. Stir in the cornflour mixture and the sherry. Heat, stirring constantly, until the mixture thickens.

5 Stir in the chopped tarragon. Add the chopped tomato with a little salt and pepper, to taste. Stir until the sauce is thoroughly combined.

6 Place the trout fillets on warmed serving plates. Spoon the sauce over and serve the fish with boiled new potatoes and green beans.

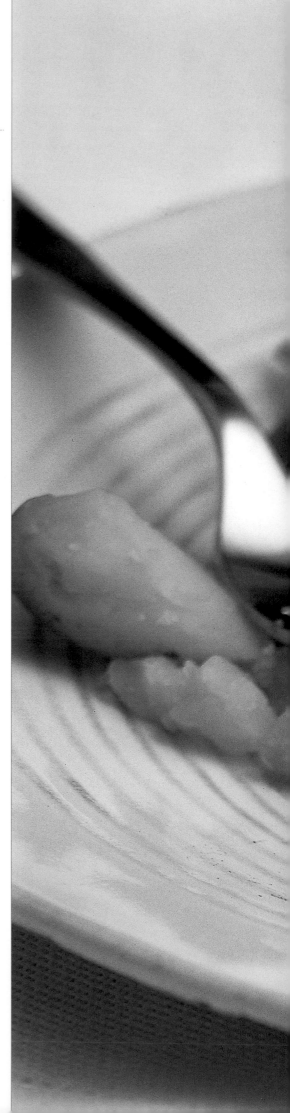

THAI-STYLE TROUT

THE COMBINATION OF CLASSIC THAI AROMATIC INGREDIENTS — GINGER, LEMON GRASS, COCONUT MILK AND LIME — GIVES THIS SIMPLE DISH A FABULOUS FLAVOUR. SERVE WITH PLENTY OF STEAMED THAI FRAGRANT RICE TO SOAK UP THE DELICIOUS SAUCE.

SERVES 4

INGREDIENTS
 200g/7oz spinach leaves
 1 lemon grass stalk, finely chopped
 2.5cm/1in piece fresh root ginger,
   peeled and finely grated
 2 garlic cloves, crushed
 200ml/7fl oz/scant 1 cup coconut milk
 30ml/2 tbsp freshly squeezed
   lime juice
 15ml/1 tbsp soft light brown sugar
 4 trout fillets, each about 200g/7oz
 salt and ground black pepper
 steamed Thai fragrant rice, to serve

COOK'S TIP
To steam Thai fragrant rice, cook it in a pan of salted boiling water for three-quarters of the time noted on the packet. Transfer it to a colander lined with muslin or cheesecloth and steam over simmering water for 5–10 minutes until just tender.

1 Preheat the oven to 200°C/400°F/ Gas 6. Place the spinach in a pan, with just the water that adheres to the leaves after washing. Cover with a lid and cook gently for 3–4 minutes until the leaves have just wilted. Drain the spinach in a colander and press it with the back of a spoon to remove any excess moisture.

2 Transfer the spinach to a mixing bowl and stir in the chopped lemon grass, grated ginger and garlic.

3 Combine the coconut milk, lime juice, sugar and seasoning in a jug (pitcher). Place the trout fillets side by side in a shallow baking dish and pour the coconut milk mixture over.

4 Bake the trout for 20–25 minutes until cooked. Place on individual serving plates, on top of the steamed Thai fragrant rice. Toss the spinach mixture in the juices remaining in the dish, spoon on top of the fish and serve.

TROUT <u>WITH</u> CRUNCHY PEPPERCORNS

BLACK, GREEN AND PINK PEPPERCORNS ADD COLOUR AND TEXTURE TO THIS DISH, AND PROVIDE AN EXPLOSION OF TASTE IN THE MOUTH WHEN CRUNCHED. SERVE THE TROUT FILLETS WITH CREAMY MASHED POTATOES SWIRLED WITH PESTO.

SERVES 4

INGREDIENTS
60ml/4 tbsp mixed peppercorns
4 trout fillets, each about 200g/7oz, skinned
60ml/4 tbsp olive oil
juice of 1 lemon
fresh basil sprigs, to garnish
mashed potato with pesto, to serve

COOK'S TIP
Stir a large spoonful of pesto into the mashed potato just before serving, leaving green swirls in the creamy potato.

1 Place the mixed peppercorns in a mortar and crush them lightly with a pestle. Continue until about half the peppercorns are broken.

2 Press one-quarter of the peppercorns on to one side of each trout fillet, using the back of a spoon.

3 Heat the oil in a griddle pan. Place the fish in the pan, coated side up, and fry for 2–3 minutes, using a spatula to press the peppercorns further into the fish as it cooks.

4 Using the spatula, turn the trout fillets over and cook for 2–3 minutes more, until cooked right through. Turn the fillets over again in the pan and sprinkle with the lemon juice.

5 Place each fish on a bed of pesto mash on an individual plate and garnish with the basil sprigs.

STUFFED TROUT WITH TARRAGON SAUCE

TARRAGON AND TROUT MAKE A MARVELLOUS TEAM. HERE WHOLE TROUT ARE FILLED WITH A HERBY STUFFING BEFORE BEING BAKED IN WINE AND SERVED WITH A CREAMY TARRAGON SAUCE. REMOVING THE SKIN BEFORE SERVING REVEALS THE ATTRACTIVE PALE PINK TROUT FLESH.

SERVES 4

INGREDIENTS

90ml/6 tbsp fresh white
    breadcrumbs
30ml/2 tbsp chopped fresh
    tarragon
1 egg, beaten
4 whole trout, each about
    200g/7oz, cleaned and boned
    for stuffing
1 small onion, sliced
150ml/¼ pint/⅔ cup dry
    white wine
8 fresh tarragon sprigs
25g/1oz/2 tbsp butter
15ml/1 tbsp plain (all-purpose) flour
150ml/¼ pint/⅔ cup single
    (light) cream
salt and ground black pepper
new potatoes and a selection of
    steamed green vegetables, to serve

COOK'S TIPS

• For a low-fat version that still tastes
delicious, use skimmed milk instead of
cream in this recipe and serve with plain
boiled potatoes.
• Fresh tarragon leaves can be infused
(steeped) in boiling water for about
10 minutes to make a refreshing tisane.

1 Preheat the oven to 190°C/375°F/
Gas 5. Mix the breadcrumbs with half
the chopped tarragon in a bowl. Season
with salt and pepper, then bind the
mixture together with the beaten egg.

2 Spread a layer of tarragon stuffing
inside the cavity of each trout,
pressing the mixture down firmly to
mould it to the shape of the cavity.
Season the trout well.

3 Place the trout in a single layer in
a shallow baking dish. Add the onion
slices and wine to the dish and top
each fish with a sprig of tarragon.
Cover the dish tightly with foil. Bake
for 20–25 minutes or until tender.

4 Carefully remove the cooked trout
from the dish, reserving the cooking
liquid. Remove the heads, tails and
skin, then place the fish in a hot
ovenproof dish. Cover with foil and
keep warm in the oven.

5 Strain the cooking liquid into a
measuring jug (cup) and if necessary
make up with water to give 150ml/
¼ pint/⅔ cup of liquid.

6 Melt the butter in a pan, stir in the
flour and cook, stirring constantly, for
1–2 minutes. Gradually add the cooking
liquid, stirring constantly. Add the
cream in the same way and bring to
the boil. Continue to stir as the mixture
thickens to a smooth sauce. Season
with salt and black pepper and add the
remaining chopped tarragon.

7 Blanch the remaining tarragon sprigs
by plunging them briefly into a pan of
boiling water. Drain well.

8 Place the trout on warmed individual
serving plates, pour over the tarragon
sauce and garnish with the blanched
tarragon sprigs. Serve with buttered new
potatoes and a selection of steamed
green vegetables.

POACHED TROUT <u>WITH</u> FENNEL

COOKING TROUT, FENNEL AND POTATOES TOGETHER IN ONE DISH MAKES FOR AN EASY SUPPER — SIMPLY ADD YOUR FAVOURITE STEAMED GREEN VEGETABLES TO COMPLETE THE MEAL.

<u>SERVES 2</u>

INGREDIENTS

    1 small fennel bulb, about 175g/6oz,
      with fronds
    25g/1oz/2 tbsp butter, plus extra
      for greasing
    350g/12oz potatoes, peeled and
      thinly sliced
    1 bay leaf
    60ml/4 tbsp dry vermouth
    60ml/4 tbsp water
    2 trout, about 225g/8oz each, cleaned
    lemon and lime slices, to garnish
    steamed green vegetables, to serve

1 Preheat the oven to 180°C/350°F/ Gas 4. Cut the feathery green fronds from the fennel, chop very finely and set aside. Slice the fennel bulb thinly.

2 Grease a shallow baking dish with butter and spread out the fennel bulb slices to cover the base of the dish.

3 Spread out the potato slices on top of the fennel and top with the bay leaf. Pour the vermouth and water over the vegetables. Season to taste.

4 Cover the dish tightly with foil and bake in the oven for 35–40 minutes.

5 Remove the dish from the oven and lift off the foil. Place the trout on top of the vegetables and dot with butter. Replace the foil and bake for 20–25 minutes more, until the trout are cooked and the vegetables are tender.

6 Remove the foil and sprinkle the reserved chopped fennel over the fish. Garnish with the lemon and lime slices. Serve immediately, with the steamed green vegetables.

COOK'S TIP
Dry vermouth has a concentrated flavour that works very well in this recipe, and the herbs that are an intrinsic part of it are more than a match for the robust flavour of the fennel.

GARLIC BAKED TROUT WITH AVOCADO SALAD

PACKED FULL OF FLAVOUR AND WITH PLENTY OF VITAMINS AND MINERALS, THIS BAKED TROUT IS
A VERSATILE MAIN DISH. SERVE IT AS SOON AS THE TROUT COMES OUT OF THE OVEN, WITH NEW
POTATOES, OR COLD WITH COUNTRY BREAD. IF THE LATTER, DRESS THE SALAD JUST BEFORE SERVING.

SERVES 4

INGREDIENTS
  6 plum tomatoes, halved
  2 garlic cloves, thinly sliced
  15g/½oz/½ cup fresh basil leaves
  45ml/3 tbsp olive oil
  4 trout fillets, each about
    200g/7oz, skinned
  2 avocados
  juice of 1 lime
  75g/3oz watercress, land cress
    or rocket (arugula)
  salt and ground black pepper
  lime wedges, to garnish

VARIATION
If you want to add extra piquancy to this
dish, serve it with a spoonful of chunky
avocado salsa. To make the salsa, halve
1 ripe avocado and remove the stone
(pit). Peel and dice the flesh and toss
in 5ml/1 tsp lemon juice, in a bowl, to
prevent the avocado browning. Dice a
2.5cm/1in piece of cucumber and add to
the avocado. Finely chop half a red chilli
and stir well so that all the ingredients
are combined. Cover with clear film
(plastic wrap) until ready to serve.

COOK'S TIP
To remove the stone from an avocado,
cut the avocado in half lengthways, then
tap the stone with the blade of a sharp
knife. When you pull the knife away from
the avocado the stone will come away
from the flesh.

1 Preheat the oven to 180°C/350°F/
Gas 4. Place the tomatoes on a baking
tray lined with baking parchment.

2 Sprinkle the garlic and basil over the
tomatoes and season well with black
pepper. Drizzle 15ml/1 tbsp of the olive
oil over and bake for 25 minutes.
Remove from the oven.

3 Using a spatula, move the tomato
halves closer together, if necessary,
to make room for the trout. Place the
fillets on the baking tray. Return the tray
to the oven for a further 15 minutes.

4 Test the fish with a fork to check it
is cooked through: if the flesh flakes
easily it is ready. Remove the baking
tray from the oven.

5 Meanwhile, cut the avocados in
half, remove the stone (pit) and peel,
then slice the flesh lengthways into
fine pieces.

6 In a small jug (pitcher), whisk the
lime juice with the remaining olive oil.
Season the dressing with salt and plenty
of ground black pepper.

7 Divide the watercress, land cress or
rocket among four individual serving
plates. Top with the avocado slices.
Drizzle the lime dressing over.

8 Using a fish slice, lift the cooked
trout fillets carefully off the baking tray
and place them on a board.

9 Arrange the cooked tomatoes over the
salad leaves and pour over any cooking
juices that have accumulated on the
baking parchment.

10 Flake the trout into bitesize pieces
and divide among the plates, arranging
it attractively amongst the salad leaves.
Garnish the plates with the lime wedges
and serve.

TROUT <u>WITH</u> ORANGE SAUCE

STUFFING TROUT WITH MUSHROOMS AND PARSLEY NOT ONLY ADDS A NEW FLAVOUR DIMENSION BUT ALSO MAKES THE MEAL MORE SUBSTANTIAL. TANGY ORANGE SAUCE IS A PERFECT ACCOMPANIMENT.

SERVES 4

INGREDIENTS

4 whole trout, each about
  175g/6oz, cleaned
25g/1oz/2 tbsp butter
1 small onion, finely chopped
50g/2oz/¾ cup button (white)
  mushrooms, chopped
25g/1oz/½ cup fresh white
  breadcrumbs
30ml/2 tbsp chopped fresh
  parsley
1 egg, beaten
juice of 2 oranges
salt and ground black pepper
fresh dill sprigs, to garnish

For the orange sauce
  25g/1oz/2 tbsp butter
  pinch of caster (superfine) sugar
  1 orange, thinly sliced
  juice of 1 orange
  juice of ½ lemon

1 Remove the heads and gills from the trout. Rinse the cavities thoroughly and bone the fish to make them easier to stuff.

2 Preheat the oven to 190°C/375°F/ Gas 5. Melt the butter in a small pan, and fry the onion over a medium heat for 4–5 minutes until translucent.

3 Add the mushrooms to the pan and fry for a further minute. Remove from the heat and stir in the breadcrumbs, parsley and egg. Season with plenty of salt and black pepper.

4 Stuff each trout with one-quarter of the mixture, pressing the mixture firmly to distribute evenly and enclose it securely in the fish.

5 Season the trout well and place in a single layer in a shallow baking dish. Pour over the orange juice. Cover the dish with foil. Cook for 20–25 minutes or until the trout are cooked through.

6 Meanwhile, make the sauce. Melt the butter in a frying pan and add the sugar. Add the orange slices to the pan and brown on both sides. Add the orange and lemon juice and stir well. Cook for 2–3 minutes, then remove from the heat.

7 Carefully lift the cooked trout out of the dish, reserving the cooking liquid. Place the fish on a hot serving dish, cover with foil and keep warm in the oven.

8 Add the cooking liquid to the sauce in the frying pan and stir well. Garnish the stuffed trout with the orange slices and dill sprigs, then pour the orange sauce over and serve.

TROUT WITH FILO PASTRY AND ALMOND CRUST

BEAUTIFUL PRESENTATION IS A REAL PLUS WHEN IT COMES TO SERVING FISH, AND THIS TROUT IS AS PRETTY AS A PICTURE WITH ITS FILO WRAPPING DUSTED WITH ALMONDS. ALMONDS ARE USED IN THE DELICIOUS STUFFING, TOO, MAKING THIS A TASTY AND FILLING MAIN COURSE.

SERVES 4

INGREDIENTS

    4 whole trout, each about
        175g/6oz, cleaned
    40g/1½oz/3 tbsp butter
    1 small onion, finely chopped
    115g/4oz/1 cup ground almonds
    30ml/2 tbsp chopped fresh
        parsley
    finely grated rind of 1 lemon
    12 sheets filo pastry
    salt and ground black pepper
    lemon slices and parsley sprigs,
        to garnish

VARIATIONS

• It is well known that almonds go particularly well with trout but you could try this recipe with other nuts too. Hazelnuts, pine nuts, pistachios and macadamias would provide an interesting variation.

• Other fresh-tasting herbs such as chervil or tarragon can be used in place of the parsley.

COOK'S TIP

Before working with filo pastry, remove it from the refrigerator and leave, still in its wrapper, for 15 minutes at room temperature. Once the filo pastry sheets have been removed from the packet, they should be covered with a damp, clean dishtowel or clear film (plastic wrap) until needed, so that they do not dry out. If they become too brittle they will not wrap easily around the fish. Any unused filo pastry can be stored in the refrigerator for up to 1 week. It would also freeze well.

1 Preheat the oven to 200°C/400°F/ Gas 6. Season the trout generously with salt and black pepper.

2 Melt 25g/1oz/2 tbsp of the butter in a large pan and cook the onion for 1–2 minutes until soft and translucent. Do not allow the onion to brown.

3 Stir 75g/3oz/¾ cup of the ground almonds into the onions in the pan, then add the chopped parsley and the lemon rind. Stir well to combine.

4 Gently stuff the cavity of each trout with one-quarter of the mixture. Press the mixture down firmly to mould it to the shape of the cavity.

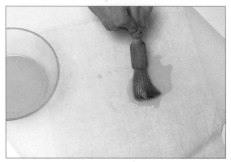

5 Melt the remaining butter. Cut three sheets of filo pastry into long strips and brush with the melted butter.

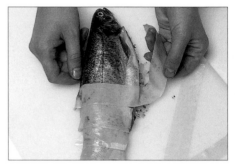

6 Wrap the strips around one fish, with the buttered side inside. Leave the head and the tail free. Place on a baking sheet. Wrap the remaining trout.

7 Brush the top of the pastry casing with melted butter and sprinkle the remaining ground almonds over the fish. Bake for 20–25 minutes until the pastry is golden brown.

8 Place on warmed individual serving dishes, garnish with the lemon slices and parsley sprigs and serve.

TROUT GOUGÈRE

A GOUGÈRE IS A CHOUX PASTRY RING FLAVOURED WITH CHEESE. THIS ONE IS SERVED HOT, WITH A RICH, CREAMY TROUT AND WATERCRESS FILLING. ALTHOUGH IT IS EASY TO PREPARE, THIS MAKES AN IMPRESSIVE LUNCH OR SUPPER DISH.

SERVES 4

INGREDIENTS
For the gougère
    50g/2oz/¼ cup butter
    150ml/¼ pint/⅔ cup water
    65g/2½oz/generous ½ cup plain
       (all-purpose) flour
    2 eggs, beaten
    75g/3oz Gruyère cheese, grated
    butter, for greasing

For the filling
    350g/12oz trout fillet
    150ml/¼ pint/⅔ cup dry white wine
    4 fresh parsley sprigs
    ½ lemon, sliced
    1 bay leaf
    25g/1oz/2 tbsp butter
    1 small onion, chopped
    25g/1oz/¼ cup plain
       (all-purpose) flour
    150ml/¼ pint/⅔ cup milk
    60ml/4 tbsp double (heavy) cream
    50g/2oz Gruyère cheese, grated
    50g/2oz watercress, finely chopped
    salt and ground black pepper

1 Preheat the oven to 200°C/400°F/ Gas 6. Sift the flour on to a sheet of non-stick baking parchment. Draw a 20cm/8in circle on a separate sheet of baking parchment. Grease a baking sheet and place the parchment on it.

2 Make the choux paste for the ring. Put the butter and water in a medium pan and heat gently until the butter melts. Bring to the boil then remove the pan from the heat.

3 Quickly tip in all the sifted flour and beat the mixture with a wooden spoon until a smooth, glossy paste forms. Leave to cool for 5 minutes.

4 Add the beaten egg to the cooled paste gradually, stirring all the time to prevent the mixture from curdling. Stir in three-quarters of the grated Gruyère cheese.

5 Carefully spoon the choux paste into a piping (pastry) bag fitted with a 1cm/½in plain round nozzle and pipe just inside the circle to form a ring. Sprinkle with the remaining cheese. Bake in the oven for 20–25 minutes or until golden brown and crisp.

6 Meanwhile, make the filling. Place the trout fillet, wine, parsley, lemon slices and bay leaf in a large frying pan. Gently poach the fish for 4–6 minutes, until it is cooked. Remove the fish from the pan. Strain the cooking liquid and reserve. Skin the fish, remove any bones and flake it into bitesize pieces.

7 Heat the butter in a pan, add the onion and fry gently for about 5 minutes until softened.

8 Stir the flour into the pan and cook for 1 minute, stirring. Gradually add the reserved cooking liquid and the milk, stirring constantly to form a thick sauce. Add the flaked trout, cream, cheese and watercress to the sauce and season well. Heat gently until piping hot.

9 When the choux ring is cooked, remove it from the oven and place on a warmed serving plate. Slice the gougère in half horizontally and spoon in the hot trout and watercress filling. Replace the pastry lid on the ring and serve immediately.

COOK'S TIP
Instead of using a piping bag, you can place large spoonfuls of choux pastry in a circle on the baking parchment. Position them close together so that they will join into a ring as they cook.

TROUT <u>AND</u> ASPARAGUS PIE

*CRISP FILO PASTRY FILLED WITH LAYERS OF TROUT, RICOTTA
CHEESE, ASPARAGUS AND MUSHROOMS MAKES A DRAMATIC-LOOKING
DISH THAT IS ABSURDLY EASY TO MAKE.*

SERVES 6–8

INGREDIENTS
  115g/4oz asparagus
  75g/3oz/6 tbsp butter
  1 small onion, chopped
  115g/4oz/1½ cups button (white)
    mushrooms, sliced
  30ml/2 tbsp chopped fresh flat
    leaf parsley
  250g/9oz/generous 1 cup ricotta
    cheese
  115g/4oz/½ cup mascarpone
    cheese
  450g/1lb trout fillet, skinned
  8 filo pastry sheets, each measuring
    45 x 25cm/18 x 10in
  salt and ground black pepper
  butter, for greasing
  flat leaf parsley, to garnish

1 Preheat the oven to 200°C/400°F/
Gas 6. Grease a 23cm/9in springform
cake tin (pan). Bring a pan of water to
the boil, add the asparagus and blanch
for 3 minutes. Drain, refresh under cold
water and drain again.

2 Heat 25g/1oz/2 tbsp of the butter in
a frying pan and add the onion. Cook
for 3–5 minutes or until softened. Add
the mushrooms and cook for 2 minutes
more. Stir in the parsley and season
well with salt and black pepper.

3 In a mixing bowl combine the ricotta
and mascarpone cheeses. Stir in the
onion mixture. Melt the remaining
butter in a small pan.

4 Line the cake tin with the filo pastry
sheets, brushing each layer with melted
butter and leaving the edges hanging
over the sides of the tin. While you are
working with one filo pastry sheet, keep
the rest covered with a damp, clean
dishtowel so that they do not dry out.

5 Place half the ricotta mixture in the
base of the filo-lined tin. Remove any
remaining pin bones from the trout
fillets, then arrange them in a single
layer over the ricotta. Season well.

6 Top with the asparagus and the
remaining ricotta mixture. Bring the
overhanging edges of the pastry over
the top, and brush the layers with the
remaining butter.

7 Bake the pie for 25 minutes or until
golden brown. Cover loosely with foil
and cook for a further 15 minutes.

8 To serve, remove the pie from the
tin and place it on a warmed serving
plate. Serve in slices, garnished with
flat leaf parsley.

RICE, NOODLES AND PASTA

You don't need a lot of trout to make an impact in a rice or pasta dish. In Trout and Prosciutto Risotto Rolls, for instance, there is just one trout fillet per person, but when that fillet is curled around a delectable prawn and risotto mixture and is itself wrapped in paper-thin ham, the results are superb. Trout is very good in pasta dishes, too, whether cold, as in Smoked Trout Pasta Salad, or hot, as in Malaysian Steamed Trout with Noodles.

TROUT WITH BLACK RICE

PINK TROUT FILLETS COOKED WITH GINGER, GARLIC AND CHILLI MAKE A STUNNING CONTRAST TO THE NUTTY BLACK RICE.

SERVES 2

INGREDIENTS

2.5cm/1in piece fresh root ginger,
  peeled and grated
1 garlic clove, crushed
1 fresh red chilli, seeded and
  finely chopped
30ml/2 tbsp soy sauce
2 trout fillets, each about 200g/7oz
oil, for greasing

For the rice
15ml/1 tbsp sesame oil
50g/2oz/¾ cup fresh shiitake
  mushrooms, sliced
8 spring onions (scallions),
  finely chopped
150g/5oz/¾ cup black rice
4 slices fresh root ginger
900ml/1½ pints/3¾ cups
  boiling water

1 Make the rice. Heat the sesame oil in a pan and fry the mushrooms with half the spring onions for 2–3 minutes.

2 Add the rice and sliced ginger to the pan and stir well. Cover with the boiling water and bring to the boil. Reduce the heat, cover and simmer for 25–30 minutes or until the rice is tender. Drain well and cover to keep warm.

COOK'S TIP
Do not have the heat too high when heating the sesame oil, as it smokes readily. If you prefer, you can mix 10ml/2 tsp groundnut (peanut) oil with 5ml/1 tsp sesame oil.

3 While the rice is cooking, preheat the oven to 200°C/400°F/Gas 6. In a small bowl mix together the grated ginger, garlic, chilli and soy sauce.

4 Place the fish, skin side up, in a lightly oiled shallow baking dish. Using a sharp knife, make several slits in the skin of the fish, then spread the ginger paste all over the fillets.

5 Cover the dish tightly with foil and cook in the oven for 20–25 minutes or until the trout fillets are cooked through.

6 Divide the rice between two warmed serving plates. Remove the ginger. Lay the fish on top and sprinkle over the reserved spring onions, to garnish.

SMOKED TROUT RISOTTO

The most important point to remember when you're making risotto is that you need to be patient. The rice needs constant stirring and once all the liquid has been absorbed it is best served straight away.

SERVES 4

INGREDIENTS

1.2 litres/2 pints/5 cups hot
  fish stock
30ml/2 tbsp olive oil
1 medium onion, finely chopped
400g/14oz/2 cups risotto rice,
  preferably arborio
150ml/¼ pint/⅔ cup dry
  white wine
45ml/3 tbsp crème fraîche or
  sour cream
45ml/3 tbsp grated Parmesan
  cheese, plus extra, to serve
350g/12oz smoked trout, roughly
  chopped
60ml/4 tbsp chopped fresh chervil
salt and ground black pepper
fresh chervil sprigs, to garnish

COOK'S TIPS
• To make Italian risotto it is essential to use a risotto rice. This special, fat short grain rice is unlike ordinary short grain rice in that it retains its texture while giving dishes a beautiful creaminess. Italian arborio rice, which originates from the Po valley region of northern Italy, is particularly favoured for its nutty flavour. This is the most widely available variety, but you may also find carnaroli and vialone nano in specialist shops, and these would also be suitable.
• For best results, use a well-flavoured fish stock. A home-made stock is best of all but you could use a good fresh stock for convenience if time is short.
• Parmesan cheese is a key ingredient in any Italian risotto. Avoid ready-grated Parmesan and opt for a chunk freshly cut off the block. It is more expensive but it will keep for a long time in the refrigerator and there is no substitute for the flavour.
• During cooking, adjust the heat so that the risotto bubbles merrily. Do not let it boil or the stock will evaporate before it can be absorbed by the rice.

1 For the creamiest risotto the stock needs to be hot when it is added to the rice, so keep it simmering in a pan on top of the stove, next to the risotto pan.

2 Heat the oil in a large pan: a paella pan or a large, heavy pan would be ideal. Add the chopped onion and fry it gently over a low heat for about 5 minutes until softened. Do not allow the onion to brown.

3 Add the rice to the pan and stir well with a wooden spoon to coat each grain thoroughly in oil. Cook over a low heat for 2–3 minutes until the rice grains have turned translucent.

4 Pour the white wine over the rice in the pan, stirring constantly. Continue to stir for 1–2 minutes until all of the wine has been absorbed.

5 Keeping the pan over a medium heat, add the hot stock, a ladleful at a time, stirring all the time.

6 Add another ladleful of stock to the rice only when the previous quantity has been absorbed, and continue in this way until all the stock has been used up. This will take around 20 minutes. As the rice cooks the mixture will thicken – the risotto is cooked when the rice has a velvety texture. When you taste them, the grains of rice should still have a bit of bite in the centre.

7 Remove the pan from the heat and stir in the crème fraîche or sour cream and the grated Parmesan cheese. Add three-quarters of the chopped smoked trout and the chopped chervil. Season with plenty of salt and black pepper and stir well to mix. Cover the pan and leave to stand for about 2 minutes.

8 Divide the risotto among four warmed serving plates, top with the remaining smoked trout and garnish with the fresh chervil sprigs. Extra grated Parmesan cheese can be offered separately.

TROUT AND PROSCIUTTO RISOTTO ROLLS

THIS MAKES A DELICIOUS AND ELEGANT MEAL. THE RISOTTO — MADE WITH PORCINI MUSHROOMS AND PRAWNS — IS A FINE MATCH FOR THE ROBUST FLAVOUR OF THE TROUT ROLLS.

SERVES 4

INGREDIENTS
    4 trout fillets, skinned
    4 slices prosciutto
    capers, to garnish

For the risotto
    30ml/2 tbsp olive oil
    8 large raw prawns (shrimp),
      peeled and deveined
    1 medium onion, chopped
    225g/8oz/generous 1 cup risotto rice
    about 105ml/7 tbsp white wine
    about 750ml/1¼ pints/3 cups
      simmering fish or chicken stock
    15g/½oz/2 tbsp dried porcini or
      chanterelle mushrooms, soaked for
      10 minutes in warm water to cover
    salt and ground black pepper

2 Add the chopped onion to the oil remaining in the pan and fry over a gentle heat for 3–4 minutes until soft. Add the rice and stir for 3–4 minutes until the grains are evenly coated in oil. Add 75ml/5 tbsp of the wine and then the stock, a little at a time, stirring over a gentle heat and allowing the rice to absorb the liquid before adding more.

4 Remove the pan from the heat and stir in the prawns. Preheat the oven to 190°C/375°F/Gas 5.

5 Take a trout fillet, place a spoonful of risotto at one end and roll up. Wrap each fillet in a slice of prosciutto and place in a greased baking dish.

1 First make the risotto. Heat the oil in a large, heavy saucepan or deep frying pan and fry the prawns very briefly until flecked with pink. Lift out with a slotted spoon and transfer to a plate.

3 Strain the mushrooms, reserving the liquid, and cut the larger ones in half. Towards the end of cooking, stir the mushrooms into the risotto with 15ml/ 1 tbsp of the reserved mushroom liquid. The rice should be soft and creamy, with just a little "bite" in the centre of the grain. If necessary, add a little more stock or mushroom liquid and cook for a few minutes more. Season to taste with salt and pepper.

6 Spoon any remaining risotto around the fish fillets and sprinkle over the rest of the wine. Cover loosely with foil and bake for 15–20 minutes until the fish is tender. Spoon the risotto on to a platter, top with the trout rolls and garnish with capers. Serve immediately.

COOK'S TIP
There are no hard and fast rules about which type of risotto to use for this dish. Almost any risotto recipe could be used, although a vegetable or seafood risotto would be particularly suitable.

TROUT WITH RICE, TOMATOES AND NUTS

THIS RECIPE COMES FROM NORTHERN SPAIN, WHERE TROUT IS VERY POPULAR. IF YOU FILLET THE FISH BEFORE YOU BAKE IT, IT COOKS MORE EVENLY AND NO BONES GET IN THE WAY OF THE STUFFING.

SERVES 4

INGREDIENTS

2 fresh trout, each about 500g/1¼lb
75g/3oz/¾ cup mixed unsalted
    cashew nuts, pine nuts, almonds
    and hazelnuts
25ml/1½ tbsp olive oil, plus extra
    for drizzling
1 small onion, finely chopped
10ml/2 tsp grated fresh root ginger
175g/6oz/1½ cups cooked white
    long grain rice
4 tomatoes, peeled and very
    finely chopped
4 sun-dried tomatoes in oil, drained
    and chopped
30ml/2 tbsp chopped fresh tarragon
2 fresh tarragon sprigs
salt and ground black pepper
dressed green leaves, to serve

3 Heat the oil in a small frying pan and fry the onion for 3–4 minutes until soft. Stir in the ginger, cook for 1 minute more, then spoon into a mixing bowl.

4 Add the rice to the mixture in the bowl, then stir in the chopped tomatoes, sun-dried tomatoes, toasted nuts and chopped tarragon. Season the stuffing with plenty of salt and black pepper.

5 Place each of the trout in turn on a large piece of oiled foil and spoon the stuffing into the cavity. Add a sprig of tarragon and a drizzle of olive oil.

6 Fold the foil over to enclose each trout and put the parcels in a large roasting pan. Bake for 20–25 minutes until the fish is tender. Cut the fish into thick slices. Serve with the green salad.

1 Using a sharp knife, fillet the trout. Check the cavity for any remaining tiny bones and remove these with tweezers.

2 Preheat the oven to 190ºC/375ºF/ Gas 5. Spread out the nuts in a baking tray and bake for 3–4 minutes, shaking the tray occasionally. Chop the nuts.

MALAYSIAN STEAMED TROUT WITH NOODLES

THIS SIMPLE DISH, SERVED ON A BED OF NOODLES, CAN BE PREPARED EXTREMELY QUICKLY. IT IS SUITABLE FOR ANY FISH FILLETS.

2 Mix together the coconut, lime rind and chopped coriander and spread one-quarter of the mixture over each trout fillet. Sandwich another trout fillet on top.

3 Mix the lime juice with the oils, adjusting the quantity of chilli oil to your own taste, and drizzle the mixture over the trout "sandwiches".

4 Prepare a steamer. Fold up the edges of the paper and pleat them over the trout to make parcels, making sure they are well sealed.

5 Place in the steamer insert and steam over the simmering water for about 10–15 minutes, depending on the thickness of the trout fillets.

6 Meanwhile, cook the noodles in a large pan of boiling water for 5–8 minutes, until just tender. Drain, toss with a little chilli oil, if you like, and divide among four warmed plates. Remove each trout "sandwich" from its wrapper and place on top of the noodles. Garnish with the lime slices and coriander.

SERVES 4

INGREDIENTS
 8 pink trout fillets of even thickness, about 115g/4oz each, skinned
 45ml/3 tbsp grated creamed coconut or desiccated (dry unsweetened shredded) coconut
 grated rind and juice of 2 limes
 45ml/3 tbsp chopped fresh coriander (cilantro)
 15ml/1 tbsp groundnut (peanut) oil
 2.5–5ml/½–1 tsp chilli oil
 350g/12oz broad egg noodles
 salt and ground black pepper
 lime slices and coriander, to garnish

VARIATION
Use the flesh from a coconut to make a tasty alternative garnish. Having rinsed the flesh with cold water, cut off thin slices using a swivel-bladed vegetable peeler. Toast the slices under a medium grill (broiler) until the coconut has curled and the edges have turned golden. Sprinkle the shavings over the trout fillets before serving.

1 Cut four rectangles of baking parchment, each about twice the size of the trout fillets. Place a fillet on each piece and season lightly.

BUCKWHEAT NOODLES <u>WITH</u> SMOKED TROUT

THE LIGHT, CRISP TEXTURE OF THE PAK CHOI BALANCES THE STRONG, EARTHY FLAVOURS OF THE MUSHROOMS AND BUCKWHEAT NOODLES AND THE SMOKINESS OF THE TROUT.

<u>SERVES 4</u>

INGREDIENTS

350g/12oz buckwheat noodles
30ml/2 tbsp vegetable oil
115g/4oz/1½ cup fresh shiitake
  mushrooms, stems trimmed,
  quartered
2 garlic cloves, finely chopped
15ml/1 tbsp grated fresh root
  ginger
225g/8oz pak choi (bok choy)
1 spring onion (scallion), finely
  sliced diagonally
15ml/1 tbsp dark sesame oil
30ml/2 tbsp mirin or sweet sherry
30ml/2 tbsp soy sauce
2 smoked trout, skinned and boned
salt and ground black pepper
30ml/2 tbsp coriander (cilantro)
  leaves and 10ml/2 tsp sesame
  seeds, toasted, to garnish

1 Cook the buckwheat noodles in a pan of boiling water for 7–10 minutes, or until just tender, following the instructions on the packet.

2 Meanwhile, heat the vegetable oil in a large frying pan. Add the shiitake mushrooms and sauté over a medium heat for 3 minutes. Add the garlic, ginger and pak choi, and continue to sauté for 2 minutes.

COOK'S TIP
Mirin is sweet, cooking sake, available from Japanese food stores.

3 Drain the noodles and add them to the vegetables in the frying pan with the spring onion, sesame oil, mirin or sherry and soy sauce. Toss the mixture thoroughly and season with salt and black pepper to taste.

4 Break the trout into bitesize pieces. Arrange the noodle mixture on individual serving plates. Place the smoked trout on top of the noodles. Garnish with coriander leaves and sesame seeds, and serve immediately.

FUSILLI <u>WITH</u> SMOKED TROUT

IN ITS CREAMY SAUCE, THE SMOKED TROUT BLENDS BEAUTIFULLY WITH THE STILL CRISP-TENDER VEGETABLES IN THIS CLASSIC PASTA DISH.

SERVES 4–6

INGREDIENTS

2 carrots, cut into matchsticks
1 leek, cut into matchsticks
2 celery sticks, cut into matchsticks
150ml/¼ pint/⅔ cup vegetable stock
225g/8oz smoked trout fillets, skinned and cut into strips
200g/7oz cream cheese
150ml/¼ pint/⅔ cup medium sweet white wine or fish stock
15ml/1 tbsp chopped fresh dill or fennel
225g/8oz/2 cups long curly fusilli or other dried pasta shapes
salt and ground black pepper
fresh dill sprigs, to garnish

3 Cook the fusilli in a pan of salted boiling water according to the instructions on the packet. When the pasta is tender, but still firm to the bite, drain it thoroughly, and return it to the pan.

4 Add the sauce, toss lightly and transfer to a serving bowl. Top with the cooked vegetables and trout. Serve immediately, garnished with the dill sprigs.

1 Put the carrot, leek and celery matchsticks into a pan and add the stock. Bring to the boil and cook quickly for 4–5 minutes, until most of the stock has evaporated. Remove from the heat and add the smoked trout.

2 Put the cream cheese and wine or fish stock into a pan over a medium heat, and whisk until smooth. Add the dill or fennel and salt and pepper.

SMOKED TROUT CANNELLONI

ONE OF THE MOST POPULAR PASTA DISHES, CANNELLONI USUALLY HAS A MEAT AND TOMATO FILLING, OR ONE BASED ON SPINACH AND RICOTTA CHEESE. SMOKED TROUT MAKES A DELICIOUS CHANGE IN THIS LOW-FAT VERSION.

SERVES 4–6

INGREDIENTS
1 large onion, finely chopped
1 garlic clove, crushed
60ml/4 tbsp vegetable stock
2 x 400g/14oz cans chopped tomatoes
2.5ml/½ tsp dried mixed herbs
1 smoked trout, about 400g/14oz, or 225g/8oz fillets
75g/3oz/½ cup frozen peas, thawed
75g/3oz/1½ cups fresh breadcrumbs
16 no pre-cook cannelloni tubes
salt and ground black pepper

For the sauce
25g/1oz/2 tbsp butter
25g/1oz/¼ cup plain (all-purpose) flour
350ml/12fl oz/1½ cups skimmed milk
freshly grated nutmeg
25ml/1½ tbsp freshly grated Parmesan cheese

1 Put the onion, garlic clove and stock in a large pan. Cover and simmer for 3 minutes. Remove the lid and cook until the stock has reduced entirely.

2 Stir in the tomatoes and dried herbs. Simmer uncovered for 10 minutes, or until the mixture is very thick.

3 Skin the trout with a sharp knife. Flake the flesh, discarding any bones. Put the fish in a bowl and add the tomato mixture, peas and breadcrumbs. Mix well, then season with salt and pepper.

4 Spoon the filling generously into the cannelloni tubes and arrange them in an ovenproof dish. Preheat the oven to 190°C/375°F/Gas 5.

5 Make the sauce. Put the butter, flour and milk into a pan and cook over a medium heat, whisking constantly, until the sauce boils and thickens. Simmer for 2–3 minutes, stirring all the time. Season to taste with salt, freshly ground black pepper and grated nutmeg.

6 Pour the sauce over the stuffed cannelloni and sprinkle with the grated Parmesan cheese. Bake for 30–45 minutes, or until the top is golden and bubbling. Serve immediately.

COOK'S TIP
Smoked trout can be bought as fillets or as whole fish. Look for them in the chiller cabinet of the supermarket.

SMOKED TROUT PASTA SALAD

*CHOOSE HOLLOW PASTA SHAPES, SUCH AS SHELLS OR PENNE, WHICH TRAP THE CREAMY FILLING,
CREATING TASTY MOUTHFULS OF TROUT, FENNEL AND SPRING ONION. THE ADDITION OF DILL IS
NOT ONLY ATTRACTIVE, BUT ALSO GIVES THIS SALAD A DISTINCTIVE ANISEED FLAVOUR.*

SERVES 8

INGREDIENTS

15g/½oz/1 tbsp butter
1 bulb fennel, finely chopped
6 spring onions (scallions), 2 very
  finely chopped and 4 thinly sliced
225g/8oz smoked trout fillets,
  skinned and flaked
45ml/3 tbsp chopped fresh dill
120ml/4fl oz/½ cup mayonnaise
10ml/2 tsp lemon juice
30ml/2 tbsp whipping cream
450g/1lb small pasta shapes,
  such as shells
salt and ground black pepper
fresh dill sprigs, to garnish

1 Melt the butter in a small frying pan.
Add the fennel and finely chopped
spring onions and fry over a medium
heat for 3–5 minutes. Transfer to a
large bowl and leave to cool slightly.

2 Add the sliced spring onions, trout,
dill, mayonnaise, lemon juice and
cream to the bowl with the fennel.
Season lightly with salt and pepper and
mix gently until well blended.

3 Bring a large pan of lightly salted
water to the boil. Add the pasta. Cook
according to the instructions on the
packet until *al dente*. Drain thoroughly
in a colander and leave to cool.

4 Add the pasta to the vegetable and
trout mixture and toss to coat evenly.
Taste for seasoning. Serve the salad
lightly chilled or at room temperature,
garnished with the sprigs of dill.

VARIATIONS
This pasta salad works well with any type
of fresh, cooked fish fillets, including
salmon. Alternatively, you can use a
200g/7oz can of tuna in water in place
of the trout.

ON THE GRILL

Anglers swear the best place to eat trout is in the open air, and if these superb recipes are anything to go by, they are probably right. All the recipes in this chapter are cooked either on the barbecue or under the grill, so that they can be enjoyed al fresco. *As the sun goes down, sit on the patio and tuck into Thai Marinated Sea Trout, Cheese-topped Trout or Trout in Wine Sauce with Plantain. Children will love the Trout Burgers, so be sure to prepare plenty.*

TROUT BURGERS

THESE HOME-MADE FISH BURGERS REALLY ARE A TREAT. THEY PROVIDE THE IDEAL WAY OF PERSUADING CHILDREN WHO CLAIM THEY DON'T LIKE FISH TO TRY IT. COOK CHILLED BURGERS ON THE BARBECUE, IF YOU PREFER, ON A LIGHTLY OILED GRILL RACK.

MAKES 8

INGREDIENTS
  350g/12oz trout fillet, skinned
  150ml/¼ pint/⅔ cup milk
  150ml/¼ pint/⅔ cup hot fish stock
  4 spring onions (scallions),
    thinly sliced
  350g/12oz cooked potatoes, peeled
  5ml/1 tsp tartare sauce
  1 egg, beaten
  50g/2oz/1 cup fresh white
    breadcrumbs
  60ml/4 tbsp semolina
  salt and ground white pepper
  vegetable oil, for shallow frying

To serve
  120ml/4fl oz/½ cup mayonnaise
  45ml/3 tbsp drained canned
    whole kernel corn
  1 red (bell) pepper, seeded
    and finely diced
  8 burger buns
  4 ripe tomatoes, sliced
  salad leaves

1 Place the trout in a frying pan with the milk, stock and spring onions. Simmer for 5 minutes or until the fish is cooked. Lift it out of the pan and set it aside. Strain the stock through a sieve into a bowl, reserving the spring onions.

COOK'S TIP
Not all children like tartare sauce. If you have any doubts about adding it to the burger mixture, you could substitute tomato ketchup instead.

2 Mash the potatoes roughly and stir in the tartare sauce, egg and breadcrumbs. Flake the trout and add the reserved spring onions. Fold into the potato mixture and season with salt and pepper.

3 Divide the potato mixture into eight and shape into burgers, using your hands. Coat thoroughly in the semolina and pat them into shape. Arrange on a plate and place in the refrigerator for 1 hour, so that they firm up.

4 In a bowl, mix the mayonnaise for serving with the corn kernels and diced red pepper.

5 Heat the oil in a frying pan and fry the burgers for 10 minutes, turning once.

6 To serve, split open the buns and spread a little of the mayonnaise over each half. Fill with a few salad leaves, a couple of tomato slices and a fish burger. Serve immediately.

CHEESE-TOPPED TROUT

*FOR THIS SIMPLE YET SOPHISTICATED SUPPER DISH, SUCCULENT STRIPS OF FILLETED TROUT ARE
TOPPED WITH A MIXTURE OF PARMESAN CHEESE, PINE NUTS, HERBS AND BREADCRUMBS BEFORE BEING
DRIZZLED WITH LEMON BUTTER AND GRILLED UNTIL TENDER.*

SERVES 4

INGREDIENTS

  50g/2oz/1 cup fresh white
    breadcrumbs
  50g/2oz Parmesan cheese, finely
    grated
  25g/1oz/⅓ cup pine nuts, chopped
  15ml/1 tbsp chopped fresh parsley
  15ml/1 tbsp chopped fresh coriander
    (cilantro)
  30ml/2 tbsp olive oil
  4 thick trout fillets, each about
    225g/8oz
  40g/1½oz/3 tbsp butter
  juice of 1 lemon
  salt and ground black pepper
  lemon slices, to garnish
  steamed baby asparagus and carrots,
    to serve

1 In a mixing bowl, combine the
breadcrumbs, Parmesan cheese, pine
nuts, parsley and coriander. Add the oil.

2 Cut each trout fillet into two strips.
Firmly press the breadcrumb mixture
on to the top of each strip of trout.

3 Preheat the grill (broiler) to high.
Grease the grill pan with 15g/½oz of
the butter. Melt the remaining butter in
a small pan and stir in the lemon juice.

4 Place the breadcrumb-topped fillets
on the greased grill pan and pour the
lemon butter over.

5 Grill (broil) the trout for 10 minutes
or until the fillets are just cooked. Place
two trout strips on each plate, garnish
with lemon slices and serve with
steamed asparagus and carrots.

VARIATIONS
• It isn't essential to use pine nuts in
the stuffing. Almonds would work well,
or you could try hazelnuts.
• If you don't have any fresh coriander
(cilantro), increase the amount of
fresh parsley.
• Dried peaches or apricots could be
chopped finely and added to the stuffing,
with perhaps a little finely grated lemon
rind to enhance the fruity flavour.

HOT AND FRAGRANT TROUT

THIS WICKEDLY HOT MARINADE COULD BE USED WITH ANY FIRM-FLESHED FISH OR MEAT. IT ALSO MAKES A WONDERFUL SPICY DIP FOR GRILLED OR BARBECUED MEAT.

SERVES 4

INGREDIENTS

2 large fresh green chillies,
   seeded and roughly chopped
5 shallots, peeled
5 garlic cloves, peeled
30ml/2 tbsp fresh lime juice
30ml/2 tbsp Thai fish sauce
15ml/1 tbsp palm sugar or light
   muscovado (molasses) sugar
4 kaffir lime leaves, rolled into
   cigarette shapes and finely sliced
2 trout, about 350g/12oz each,
   cleaned

VARIATION
Slightly sweet coconut rice is the perfect accompaniment to this spicy trout. To make it, simply substitute coconut milk for half of the water in your usual rice recipe. Ready-to-use coconut milk is available in cartons and cans but you can make your own using a block of creamed coconut. Dissolve one 200g/7oz block creamed coconut in 400ml/14fl oz/1⅔ cup hot water. Use this amount for coconut rice for four people. If you don't use the whole block of creamed coconut, store the remainder in the refrigerator.

1 Wrap the green chillies, shallots and garlic cloves in a foil package. Place under a hot grill (broiler) for 10 minutes, until the vegetables have softened.

2 As soon as the foil package is cool enough to handle, unwrap it and tip the contents into a mortar or food processor. Blend to a paste. Add the lime juice, fish sauce, sugar and lime leaves and mix well.

3 With a teaspoon, stuff this paste inside the fish. Smear a little on the skin too. Grill (broil) the fish for about 5 minutes on each side, until just cooked through. Carefully lift the fish on to a platter. Serve with rice.

COOK'S TIPS
• Thai fish sauce (*nam pla*) is made from anchovies, which are salted, then fermented in wooden barrels. The sauce, which is ubiquitous in Thai cooking, accentuates the flavour of food.
• Kaffir lime leaves release a distinctive lemony flavour when roughly chopped or torn. They are obtainable in Asian food stores. They will keep for several days, or can be frozen.

TROUT ᴵᴺ WINE SAUCE ᵂᴵᵀᴴ PLANTAIN

IN THE WEST INDIES, WHERE THIS RECIPE ORIGINATED, THE FISH USED WOULD PROBABLY BE DOLPHINFISH OR SNAPPER, BUT THIS IS ALSO A WONDERFUL TREATMENT FOR TROUT.

SERVES 4

INGREDIENTS
4 trout fillets
15ml/1 tbsp crushed garlic
7.5ml/1½ tsp coarse-grain black pepper
7.5ml/1½ tsp paprika
7.5ml/1½ tsp celery salt
7.5ml/1½ tsp curry powder
5ml/1 tsp caster (superfine) sugar
25g/1oz/2 tbsp butter
150ml/¼ pint/⅔ cup white wine
150ml/¼ pint/⅔ cup fish stock
10ml/2 tsp clear honey
15–30ml/1–2 tbsp chopped fresh
  parsley
1 yellow plantain
oil, for frying

1 Put the trout fillets in a dish. Mix the garlic, pepper, paprika, celery salt, curry powder and sugar in a bowl. Sprinkle over the trout and marinate for 1 hour.

2 Melt the butter in a large frying pan and sauté the marinated trout fillets, in batches if necessary, for about 5 minutes or until cooked through, turning once. Transfer to a warm plate and keep hot.

3 Add the wine, fish stock and honey to the pan. Bring to the boil and simmer to reduce slightly. Return the fillets to the pan and spoon over the sauce. Sprinkle with parsley and simmer gently for a few minutes.

4 Peel the plantain and cut it into rounds. Heat a little oil in a frying pan and fry the plantain until soft and golden brown, turning once.

5 Transfer the fish to warmed serving plates, stir the sauce and pour it over. Garnish with the fried plantain.

COOK'S TIP
This recipe can also be prepared on a barbecue. Cook the fish and wine sauce in a frying pan but wrap the unpeeled plantain in foil and bake it on the barbecue for about 10 minutes, or until tender, before cutting it into rounds.

THAI MARINATED SEA TROUT

SEA TROUT HAS A SUPERB TEXTURE AND A FLAVOUR LIKE THAT OF WILD SALMON. IT IS BEST SERVED WITH STRONG BUT COMPLEMENTARY FLAVOURS, SUCH AS CHILLIES AND LIME, THAT CUT THE RICHNESS OF ITS FLESH.

SERVES 6

INGREDIENTS

   6 sea trout cutlets, each about
     115g/4oz, or wild or farmed salmon
   2 garlic cloves, chopped
   1 fresh long red chilli, seeded
     and chopped
   45ml/3 tbsp chopped Thai basil
   15ml/1 tbsp palm sugar or
     granulated sugar
   3 limes
   400ml/14fl oz/1²⁄₃ cups
     coconut milk
   15ml/1 tbsp Thai fish sauce

1 Place the sea trout cutlets side by side in a shallow dish. Using a pestle, pound the garlic and chilli in a large mortar to break both up roughly. Add 30ml/2 tbsp of the Thai basil with the sugar and continue to pound to a rough paste.

2 Grate the rind from 1 lime and squeeze it. Mix the rind and juice into the chilli paste, with the coconut milk. Pour the mixture over the cutlets. Cover and chill for about 1 hour. Cut the remaining limes into wedges.

3 Take the fish out of the refrigerator so that it can return to room temperature. Remove the cutlets from the marinade and place them in an oiled hinged wire fish basket or directly on the lightly oiled grill. Cook the fish for 4 minutes on each side, trying not to move them. They may stick to the grill rack if not seared first.

4 Strain the remaining marinade into a pan, reserving the contents of the sieve. Bring the marinade to the boil, then simmer gently for 5 minutes, stirring. Stir in the contents of the sieve and continue to simmer for 1 minute more. Add the Thai fish sauce and the remaining Thai basil.

5 Lift each fish cutlet on to a plate, pour over the sauce and serve with the lime wedges.

COOK'S TIP
Sea trout is best cooked when the barbecue is cool to medium hot, and the coals have a medium to thick coating of ash. Always remember to oil the barbecue rack or hinged grill lightly and take care when cooking any fish in a marinade, as the residue can cause flare-ups if it drips on to the coals.

BACON-WRAPPED TROUT WITH OATMEAL

THIS STUFFING IS BASED ON A SCOTTISH SPECIALITY, CALLED SKIRLIE, WHICH IS A MIXTURE OF OATMEAL AND ONION. COOK THIS TROUT ON A MEDIUM-HOT BARBECUE, IF YOU LIKE. BRUSH THE TROUT WITH OIL AND PUT IT IN A HINGED WIRE BARBECUE FISH BASKET TO MAKE IT EASIER TO TURN.

SERVES 4

INGREDIENTS
   10 dry-cured streaky bacon rashers
      (fatty bacon slices)
   40g/1½oz/3 tbsp butter or bacon fat
   1 onion, finely chopped
   115g/4oz/1 cup oatmeal
   30ml/2 tbsp chopped fresh parsley
   30ml/2 tbsp chopped fresh chives
   4 trout, each about 350g/12oz,
      cleaned and boned
   juice of ½ lemon
   salt and ground black pepper
   watercress, cherry tomatoes and
      lemon wedges, to serve

For the herb mayonnaise
   6 watercress sprigs
   15ml/1 tbsp chopped fresh chives
   30ml/2 tbsp roughly chopped fresh
      parsley
   90ml/6 tbsp lemon mayonnaise
   30ml/2 tbsp fromage frais, crème
      fraîche or sour cream
   2.5–5ml/½–1 tsp tarragon mustard

1 Preheat the oven to 190°C/375°F/ Gas 5. Chop two of the bacon rashers. Melt 25g/1oz/2 tbsp of the butter or bacon fat in a large frying pan and cook the chopped bacon briefly. Add the finely chopped onion and fry gently for 5–8 minutes, until softened.

2 Add the oatmeal and cook until the oatmeal darkens and absorbs the fat, but do not allow it to overbrown. Stir in the parsley and chives, with salt and pepper to taste. Cool.

3 Wash and dry the trout, then stuff with the oatmeal mixture. Wrap each fish in two bacon rashers and place in an ovenproof dish. Dot with the remaining butter and sprinkle with the lemon juice. Bake for 20–25 minutes, until the bacon browns and crisps a little.

4 Meanwhile, make the mayonnaise. Place the watercress, chives and parsley in a sieve and pour boiling water over them. Drain, rinse under cold water, and drain well on kitchen paper.

5 Purée the herbs in a mortar with a pestle. (This is easier than using a food processor for a quantity as small as this.) Stir the puréed herbs into the lemon mayonnaise with the fromage frais, crème fraîche or sour cream. Add tarragon mustard to taste and stir well.

6 When cooked, transfer the trout to warmed serving plates. Serve with watercress, cherry tomatoes and lemon wedges, accompanied by the herb mayonnaise.

USEFUL INFORMATION

INFORMATION SERVICES

For more information about trout, the following organizations may be helpful:

United Kingdom
British Trout Association
8–9 Lambton Place
London W11 2SH
Tel: 020 7221 6065
www.britishtrout.co.uk

Fleetwood Fish Merchants
    Association Limited
6 Station Road
Fleetwood
Lancs FY7 6NW
Tel: 01253 873358

Marine Conservation Society
9 Gloucester Road
Ross-on-Wye
Herefordshire HR9 5BU
Tel: 01989 566017
www.mcsuk.org
(If you are concerned about choosing eco-friendly fish when shopping or eating out, the Marine Conservation Society publishes a Good Fish Guide)

The Salmon & Trout Association
Fishmongers' Hall
London Bridge
London EC4R 9EL
Tel: 020 7283 5838

Wild Trout Trust
www.wildtrout.org

New Zealand Trade
    Development Board
New Zealand House
80 Haymarket
London SW1Y 4TE
Tel: 020 7973 0380
Fax: 020 7973 0104

United States
Bureau of Seafood & Aquaculture
    Marketing
2061 East Dirac Drive
Tallahassee
Florida 32310
Tel: (850) 488-0163
www.fl-seafood.com

Norwegian Seafood Export
    Council
Flagship Wharf, Suite 600
197 Eighth Street
Charlestown
MA 02129
Tel: 1-888-NORSKFISH
www.seafoodfromnorway.com/usa

Australia
Sydney Fish Markets
Gipps Street
Pyrmont NSW 2009
Tel: (02) 9660 3652

New Zealand
New Zealand Fishing
    Industry Board
Private Bag 24091
Manners Street Post Office
Wellington
Tel: (04) 385 4005/8115
www.seafood.co.nz

MAIL ORDER COMPANIES

United Kingdom
Graig Farm Organics
Tel: 01597 851655
www.graigfarm.co.uk

Atlantic Harvest Limited
Pennyburn Industrial Estate
Buncrana Road
Londonderry
Co Londonderry
BT48 0LU
Tel: 028 7126 4275

Atlantis Smoked Fish
Fore Street
Grampound
Truro
Cornwall TR2 4SB
Tel: 01726 883201

Bridfish
Unit 1
The Old Laundry Industrial Estate
Sea Road North
Bridport
Dorset DT6 3BD
Tel: 01308 456306
(Smoked trout)

Cornish Smoked Fish
    Company Limited
Charlestown
St Austell
Cornwall PL25 3NY
Tel: 01726 72356
Fax: 01726 72360

Rhydlewis Fishery
Rhydlewis
Llandysul
Ceredigion SA44 5QS
Tel/Fax: 01239 851224

United States
Always Fresh Fish
1889 Hwy 9, Unit 41
Toms River
NJ 08755
Tel: 732 349-0518
www.alwaysfreshfish.com

Australia
Aquatas Pty Limited
Marina Drive
Margate
Tasmania 7054
Tel: (03) 6267 6767
Fax: (03) 6267 9408
www.aquatas.com

Cairns Fish Marketing Agency
PO Box 201B
Bungalow
Cairns
Queensland 4870
Tel. (61) 7 40318455
Fax: (61) 7 40318355
www.cfma.com.au

Sydney Fish Market Pty Ltd
Locked Bag 247
Bank Street
Pyrmont
NSW 2009
Tel: (61) 2 9004 1100
Fax: (61) 2 9004 1177
www.sydneyfishmarket.com.au

New Zealand
New Zealand Fishing
   Industry Board
Private Bag 24091
Manners Street Post Office
Wellington
Tel: (04) 385 4005/8115
www.seafood.co.nz

GLOSSARY

Adipose fin Small fin between the dorsal fin and the tail tin on the back of a trout or salmon.

Anadromous Describes fish that migrate from the sea to fresh water to spawn. This contrasts with catadromous, which refers to fish like eels, which leave their fresh water habitat to spawn in the sea.

Anal fin A fairly large single fin close to the tail on the underbelly of a trout or salmon.

Cock trout Adult male. The term is also used for salmon.

Dapping A technique used in fly fishing, which involves suspending an imitation fly from a long rod so that it blows in the breeze before being delicately dropped, or dapped on to the water, imitating nature so expertly that the fish is fooled into thinking it is a real insect.

Dorsal fin Single large fin on the back of a trout or salmon.

Fry A very young trout or salmon, whose digestive tract has matured to allow it to feed naturally.

Hen trout Adult female. Female salmon are also called hens.

Parr Immature trout are called parr. When they are several months old, young salmon become known as parr, the name being a reference to the finger-like markings they acquire on their flanks at this time – parr being an Old English word for finger.

Pectoral fin One of a pair of fins on the underbelly of the trout or salmon, near the head.

Pelvic fin One of a pair of fins on the underbelly of the fish, more or less immediately below the dorsal fin.

Redds Gravel pits on the riverbed where trout and salmon are spawned. The female fish hide their eggs in the redds and the young trout emerge around 30 days later.

Smolt The name given to anadromous trout.

INDEX